Contents

D1386829

Controlled assessment

Controlled assessment is the new coursework. The main differences between controlled assessment and previous coursework are that:

- the tasks you choose must be from the list of AQA externally set tasks
- you will have to complete some parts of the work in the classroom at a time set by your teacher.

For the AQA GCSE Child Development course, you need to complete two controlled assessment tasks:

- one research task
- one child study.

The research task forms 20 per cent of your final mark. The child study forms 40 per cent of your final mark. The other 40 per cent of the final mark will come from the written exam.

For both controlled assessments, you will be able to research for homework. For example, you will carry out your visits in your child study and make notes on these in your own time. However, you will write up the visit in school. You could also plan and carry out questionnaires and then bring the completed sheets into school to analyse, evaluate and present the results. Your teacher will keep all your rough notes and initial research in a folder.

There are important guidelines to follow when doing this work:

- The work you hand in must be your own.
- You must not loan your work to any other candidates.
- You must not copy from other people's work (plagiarism).
- Any information copied directly from books, websites, etc. should be referenced.
- You must not hand in work that has been written or typed by another person unless this is acknowledged.

If you are absent when class time is used for the controlled assessments, your teacher will give you the chance to make up this time.

Unit 2: the research task

This is the shorter of the two tasks. You have to choose one of the AQA externally set tasks to research and investigate. These tasks are based on the following areas:

- parenthood
- pregnancy
- diet, health and care of the child
- support for the parent and child.

In these tasks, you will be expected to show the following skills:

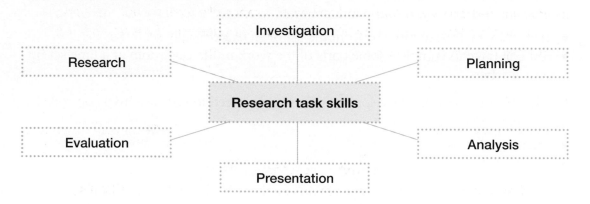

Unit 3: the child study

This is the longer of the two tasks and is designed to show your knowledge and understanding of how children develop and learn new skills. Although you choose the child you are going to study, you will have to choose one of the AQA externally set tasks for your child study task.

In the child study, you will need to show the following skills:

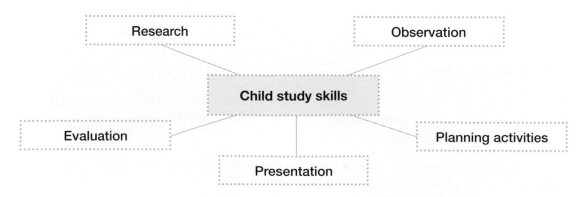

The aim of this book is to help you to understand how to work on these studies and to give you ideas that will help you to improve your chances of getting higher marks.

Skills for success

2

In both controlled assessments – the research task and the child study – you will need to show that you can use different skills to carry out the work. This section looks at some of the skills you might use and gives you tips on how to use them.

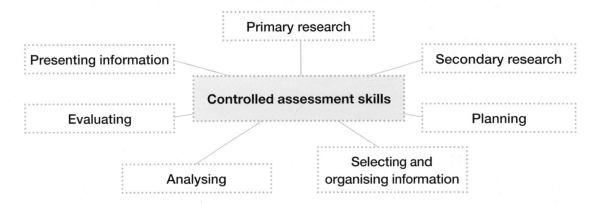

Research

Research means finding out information that helps you to understand and carry out the task you have chosen. Research is one of the most important parts of both your research task and your child study. There are two different types of research:

- **Secondary research** – this is research that may help you but that other people have already done, e.g. information from a textbook or from a website.
- **Primary research** – this is your own information that you have collected yourself, e.g. from questionnaires or from observing a child.

Secondary research

This is information that already exists. The diagram below gives you some idea of the different kinds of secondary research.

Books and magazines

Textbooks from your child development area will give you a lot of information but do not forget that books from other areas might help as well. Try your school learning resource centre and local library. Ask the librarian and they will help you search for information.

TV programmes and DVDs

Look out for useful programmes on TV, such as factual programmes or documentaries, e.g. 'Supernanny'. Children's TV channels have lots of programmes for young children and these, as well as DVDs, can give you ideas for activities or help you to understand how children learn.

Leaflets, booklets, etc.

You can get these from supermarkets, health centres, clinics, chemists, dentists, etc. These will usually give up-to-date information because they are re-printed regularly.

Secondary research

Packets, boxes and labels

You may find useful information on the packaging used for toys, nappies, baby foods, equipment, etc.

Newspapers and magazines

You can often find useful articles and news reports that might help with your research. If your family do not buy a paper, you can find newspapers in libraries. You can often find back copies (old copies) there as well. A lot of newspapers are also available on the internet.

Internet

You can find a lot of information on a wide range of subjects on the internet, but it can take a lot of time to go through all the information you find and not all of it will be relevant! You will need to spend time sorting through the information and choosing what is useful. Do not just print off everything you find.

Research does not mean just copying huge chunks of information from a textbook or printing off lots of information from a website. You need to:

→ select (pick out) what you think is important and useful

→ present it in an interesting and varied way

→ try to put it in your own words

→ evaluate it (say what you have learnt from it that is important and will help you in some way).

The next section gives you more information and ideas about some of the different types of secondary research.

Textbooks

Textbooks are an excellent resource for finding out factual information. Looking at the contents page at the front of the book or in the more detailed index at the back of the book is a quick way to find what you need.

You do not always have to read the whole book or even a chapter to find sections that will be useful to your area of research – look out for the headings.

You could look up the same information, e.g. imaginative play, in more than one book to get different ideas.

✓ **top tips**

Don't copy the same information out several times – select the most important bits and put it into a table or chart in your own words.

Try to use books that have been written recently – they will have more up-to-date information.

! **Remember**

Make a note of the title of the book and the name of the author so that you can source your information.

The internet

The easiest and quickest way to find information is to use a search engine such as www.google.co.uk or www.ask.co.uk. Just type in words or phrases related to the topic you are looking for (you can miss out joining words such as 'the' and 'of') and you will get a search results page with links to different websites. Try to stick to UK websites so that your information is relevant.

You can bookmark the most useful websites or add them to your favourites list so that they are easier to access.

Finding information is easy but it is how you use it that is important.

- Don't just print out everything and put it into your coursework as your own work – this will not get you good marks (see referencing and plagiarism on page 26).
- Use a highlighter pen on printouts and then write up the information in your own words. Alternatively, you could cut and paste important sections into a Microsoft Word document and then annotate (add notes) and evaluate it.
- Don't forget to reference the websites you have used!

> **! Remember**
>
> Try to keep a record of the websites you have used, as well as the topic you were researching. Make a note of how **useful** the information is. This will save you time later on. If you print out any information, highlight the website address.

Magazines and newspapers

You could include articles from magazines and newspapers as part of your research. Just remember to annotate and evaluate them.

Packaging and labels

Packaging used on food, toys, equipment and clothing can also provide useful information. You could cut out the packaging, stick them onto pages in your controlled assessment task and add notes to highlight important or useful information. You should then analyse what you have found out.

TV and DVDs

Many programmes on TV can be useful sources of information, from documentaries to children's programmes and soaps. However, it can be very difficult to watch a factual programme on TV and make notes at the same time, unless you have recorded the programme or have live pause and rewind. It is often easier to make a note of what you have watched at the end, with the name of the programme and the date.

Leaflets and booklets

Leaflets and booklets are usually free and will give you:

- lots of useful factual information on a wide range of topics
- ideas on how to present information in an interesting way – useful especially for the research task
- useful photos and pictures.

Primary research

This is information you collect yourself which does not already exist. The diagram below gives you some idea of the different kinds of primary research.

Questionnaires and surveys: These can be used for lots of different topics and tasks and will provide a lot of useful information about people's ideas and opinions *but* you have to plan them carefully and analyse and evaluate them thoroughly.

Visits: You could arrange to visit a nursery, health centre, toy shop, museum or play area, depending on what your task is.

Comparative investigations: These are a great way to carry out primary research. Your teacher might organise opportunities to do this during lesson time, e.g. to test how absorbent nappies are.

Emails: Emails are often now used instead of letters and could be used to send out questionnaires or to get information from experts. They are much quicker but not everyone will reply to them.

Interviews: Interviews could be used to find out the ideas, experiences and opinions from people such as midwives, new mums or nursery nurses.

Primary research

Photographs: A digital camera is great for recording evidence to use in both your research task and child study task. Including photographs in your work is quick and easy and makes it look much more interesting and professional.

Personal experiences: You can use your own ideas, experiences and memories.

Observations: This is one of the most important parts of the child study. Observations involve watching and making notes.

Risk assessments: Any activity you do with a child must be safe – a risk assessment will help you to identify possible dangers and reduce the risk of accidents. You could also use these in your research task, depending on the task you have chosen.

Inventories: These are lists of items, e.g. toys, books, types of nappies, etc. However, they are often used to compare different features of the items in the list.

The next section looks at some of these ideas in more detail.

Surveys

A survey is another way of collecting information and is usually done by either using a questionnaire or carrying out an interview. You can use a survey to find out either:

- people's opinions about something, e.g. how important books are in helping children's development, or
- factual information, e.g. what home safety devices are on sale and how much they cost.

Questionnaires

A questionnaire is a set of written questions given to a number of different people to collect information. Questionnaires need to be carefully planned.

Planning a questionnaire

- Before you start to think of questions, make sure you know exactly what you want to find out and why! How will it help you in your task?
- Try to make a prediction of what you think your questionnaire or survey will show, e.g. 'parents do not let children do much creative play because it is too messy'.
- Decide who you will ask – only ask people who can give you the information you need. For example, if you want to find out about views on pain relief during labour and birth, it would be best to ask a midwife or women who have already had children.

Then:

- Think about your questions – make them simple, clear and easy to answer.
- Do not ask too many questions because this will make it more difficult to analyse the answers. Choose five or six good questions, leaving out those that might not be important.

Then:

- Give your questionnaire a title.
- Include a brief introduction to explain clearly who you are and why you are doing the questionnaire.
- Ask your teacher to check your questionnaire before you hand it out.

Think about

How will you carry out your questionnaire? There are a few options:

1. Hand out the questionnaires and collect them in later. This is an easy option, but people may not bother to fill them in. You might have to remind people.

2. Fill in the questionnaires face-to-face as in an interview. However, this can take a lot of time.

3. Phone people. This takes a long time and you have to pay for the call.

4. Use email. Again, this is easy, but people might not bother to reply.

5. Send the questionnaires by post. You would need to include a stamped addressed envelope for people to return their questionnaires, otherwise they might not reply at all. This method also takes a lot of time.

6. A mixture of all the above.

Finally, how many people will you ask? Try to ask at least ten people because this will give you better results than if you asked just a few people.

Remember

It is OK for you to work with others to plan a questionnaire or survey and collect the information – this will give you more and better results. However, when you write up and analyse and evaluate your results, it *must* be in your own words!

Types of questions

There are two types of questions: closed and open.

Closed questions limit the possible answers because you can usually answer them by circling a word, with a short phrase or by ticking a box. They are easier to analyse than open questions and can be used to produce good graphs, charts, etc. Look at the following examples.

Example 1:

Does your child go to nursery?

Yes / No

This is quick to complete and easy to analyse.

Example 2:

> How often do you take your child to the park? Tick one.
> Every day ☐
> Once a week ☐
> Once a month ☐
> Very rarely ☐
> Never ☐

Using tick boxes, you can give a range of possible answers but can limit the choice to one. Again they are quick to fill in and easy to analyse.

Example 3:

> Which of the following toys does your child play with most regularly?
> Please tick three.
>
> | | | | |
> |---|---|---|---|
> | Jigsaw | ☐ | Soft toys | ☐ |
> | Lego® | ☐ | Board games | ☐ |
> | Dolls | ☐ | Books | ☐ |
> | Tricycle | ☐ | Pretend toys | ☐ |
> | Play dough | ☐ | Dressing up | ☐ |
> | Shops | ☐ | Paints/crayons | ☐ |
> | Balls | ☐ | Small world | ☐ |

Again this is quick to fill in and gives people more choices, but it can take longer to analyse.

Open questions ask people about their ideas and opinions but beware – they are more difficult to analyse than closed questions because 20 different people may give 20 different answers. However, they can give you more useful and detailed information.

Example 4:

> Why do you think it is important to spend time reading with your child?
>
> _____
>
> _____
>
> _____
>
> _____

top tips

Try to fit your questions onto one sheet of A4 paper. People are more likely to fill in one sheet of questions than two or more!

Once you have collected together the results of your questionnaires, you need to analyse them and present your results. You need to decide how you will use your information in the rest of your work (see page 18).

Remember

Only include one copy of your questionnaire with your work.

Interviews

An interview is one-to-one primary research.

You can use a questionnaire as an interview but usually you use an interview when you want to get more detailed or specialist information, e.g. interviewing a midwife about pain relief during labour and birth or a nursery nurse about how the nursery encourages creative play.

Like all good primary research, it needs to be planned carefully and in a similar way to a questionnaire.

Planning an interview

- Firstly, make a list of what you want to find out before you decide on the questions.
- If you are interviewing more than one person about the same topic, you need to use structured questions (e.g. closed questions; see page 9) so that you can compare and evaluate their answers.
- If you are going to interview only one person, you can use more open-ended questions (see page 10). This lets the person being interviewed talk more freely. Also, if they say something that you did not expect or think about, you can ask them more about it. This way you might get more useful information.
- Think about where you are going to carry out the interview – you need a quiet, comfortable place where you will not be interrupted.
- Plan how you will record your interview. If you try to write down everything that is said, you may miss important points and will not be able to concentrate on the answer.

Finally, you need to write up the interview and analyse it before deciding how you might use some of the information in the rest of your work (see page 22).

Inventories

An inventory is simply a list of items, such as:

- toys
- games
- books
- safety equipment
- nappies.

However, you can develop and use an inventory to make it into an easy way of collecting information, so that you can compare and analyse a range of ideas about the items.

 Think about

You will need to plan:
- what you want to find out
- how you will record your information.

The easiest way to collect the information is to use a chart. Look at the example below.

Type of toy	Age range	P	I	E	S	Any other information
Duplo®	18+ months	☺☺☺	☺	☺☺		Easy to wash Does not break easily
Soft toys						Washable
Jigsaw						Ten pieces, wooden

☺	Poor
☺☺	Good
☺☺☺	Very good

Example of an inventory

Comparative investigations

A comparative investigation can be used if you want to compare items such as different books, nappies or activities to try to identify similarities and differences.

For example, if you wanted to compare different books for the age of the child you are studying, you might want to compare:

- age range
- costs
- number of pages
- illustrations
- size of book
- ease of turning pages
- type of book.

Again you need to plan a chart so that it is easy to record your information.

	The Tiger Who Came To Tea	**The Very Hungry Caterpillar**	**Mr Grumpy**
Age range	2 years +	9 months–2 years	3 years +
Cost	£5.99	£5.99	£2.50
Number of pages	32	26	32
Size	A4	18x12 cm	14x14 cm
Ease of turning pages	Quite easy because quite big	Easy because made from card	Difficult because paper is thin
Text	Quite detailed sentences	Simple and short	Detailed sentences
Type of book	Story book	Story book	Story book
Illustrations	Clear, large and colourful	Colourful and clear drawings	Simple drawings, mainly primary colours
Special features	Some pictures have textures so help sensory skills	Cut-out holes Pop-up butterfly	None
Overall rating	☆☆☆	☆☆☆	★★

Excellent ☆☆☆
Good ★★
Poor ★

Example of a comparative investigation about children's books

> **! Remember**
>
> Like questionnaires, comparative investigations need to be analysed and evaluated (see page 22).

Risk assessments

A risk assessment is used to:

- think of (identify) any possible dangers or hazards
- decide whether these are high, medium or low risk
- decide what steps you would take to prevent them.

Risk assessments are used in industry, hospitals and schools, but could also be used in your child study when:

- looking at safety issues – e.g. safety of toys, the home
- planning visits, e.g. trips to the park, beach, swimming baths
- organising practical activities, e.g. junk modelling, cooking.

As with other types of primary research, you need to plan how you are going to record your information.

Assessment of: Date:					
Purpose of the assessment					
Possible risks	Why it is dangerous	**Level of risk**			How it can be prevented
		High	Medium	Low	

Example of a risk assessment

Observations

These are mainly used in the child study. Observing, watching and recording how children play and behave can help you to understand how they are learning and developing.

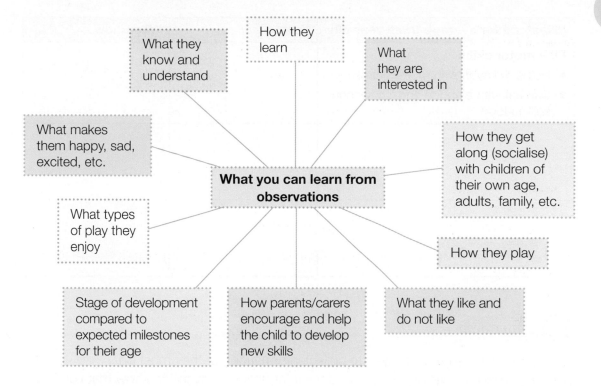

You will need to plan how to record your information. It can be difficult to play with the child and write down what you see at the same time, but you must make some notes about the visit, the activities you did with the child and how they played, so that you can write these up at a later date. You will have to keep these notes in your folder at school.

top tip

Don't rely just on your memory of the visit!

Use a notebook to write down what you have seen – make notes on how the child played, their actions and behaviour when doing different activities and how they did them.

Using bullet points can be a quick way of doing this. For example:

- Eve opened door – big hug, smile.
- Took me to see her new book.
- Read book with her – already knows it off by heart.
- Told her we were making cakes – excited.
- Helped me find the bowls. Knew 'big' and 'little'.

You could also use a simple checklist of milestones from a textbook. These could be put into chart form and you could use ticks or crosses when these have been observed.

Milestone for average three-year-old	Yes/no	When/how
Fine motor skills • Holds a crayon with more control • Can eat with a spoon and fork without spilling food		

Example of a milestone checklist

 Remember

> Checklists are a useful way to collect information but they must be explained in your own words and the information analysed to show that you understand the stage of development your child has reached.

Your observations should be quite detailed and factual. You can write up your observations either by hand or using ICT.

Analysis and evaluation

Analysis and evaluation are both very important parts of controlled assessments but they are the parts that many people find the most difficult, mainly because it can be hard to understand the difference between them.

Your teacher will help you to develop your skills in analysing and evaluating but the following might help you to develop these.

Usually **analysis** is factual – it is where you look in detail at the information or research you have produced (e.g. the results of a questionnaire or information about the importance of play) and summarise the most important points.

Evaluation often follows the analysis so is the next step – it is your own personal summary or conclusion about what is important and why. In an evaluation, you should support your ideas and opinions with quotes and references.

So let's look at where and when you might need to analyse and evaluate, and then at how to do it.

Research task	Child study
What? Analyse the research task. **Why?** To show that you understand what you need to do and to help with planning.	**What?** Analyse the introductory visit. **Why?** To summarise the stages of physical, intellectual and social development you think your child has reached and to help you decide which AQA externally set task to choose.
What? Analyse each piece of primary and secondary research. **Why?** To pick out what you think is the most important and useful information, and why.	**What?** Analyse each piece of primary and secondary research. **Why?** To pick out what you think is the most important and useful information, and why.
What? Evaluate all your research. **Why?** To summarise all your research to help you decide on your final outcome and help with planning it.	**What?** Evaluate all your research. **Why?** To help you decide activities to plan and carry out in two of your visits that will encourage development.
What? Analyse a leaflet, booklet, PowerPoint presentation. **Why?** To help you decide on what makes a good outcome.	**What**? Assess and evaluate the activities you have planned and what you have observed in each of the four visits. **Why?** To see how the child is developing and how this compares with the 'average', 'norm' or 'expected' development for a child of this age.
What? Analyse and evaluate your outcome. **Why?** To decide whether what you have made is 'fit for purpose' and satisfies the requirements of the original task *and* to explain if you made the right choices when planning and doing your task.	**What?** Analyse and evaluate the child's development at the end of the study and how successful your activities and planning have been. **Why?** To see how the child has developed since the start of the study, when you noticed important changes and how the research and activities you chose have helped development. Again you need to say how the child compares with the 'average', 'norm' or 'expected' development for a child of this age.

Analysis and evaluation of the research task and child study

The next section shows some examples of analysis and evaluation for different types of research.

Analysing questionnaires and surveys

Once you have carried out your questionnaire or survey, you need to collect and organise your results. The best way to do this is on a spreadsheet – that way you can produce charts and graphs more easily. However you can also use a tally chart, which you write out yourself.

Reply no.	Does your child go to nursery?	How often do you take your child to the park?	How important do you think it is that your child mixes with other people?
1	Yes	Never	Not very
2	Yes	Once a week	Very
3	No	Once a week	Very
4	Yes	Once a month	Very
5	No	Once a month	Very
6	Yes	Once a month	Quite
7	No	Rarely	Very
8	Yes	Never	Not very
9	Yes	Once a week	Very
10	No	Never	Very

Example of a spreadsheet

Question:

Which of the following does your child play with most regularly? Please tick three.

Jigsaws	Small world toys	Paints and crayons	Play dough	Duplo® or Lego®	Dolls	Dressing up	Pretend toys, e.g. kitchen
ЖИ III	ЖИ IIII	ЖИ	ЖИ I	ЖИ IIII II	ЖИ	III	ЖИ ЖИ III

Example of a tally chart

When you have sorted out all your results, onto either a spreadsheet or a tally chart, you can then start to analyse them. Try to present the results in a clear, colourful way, using graphs and charts.

top tips

- Make sure you choose graphs or charts that are clear and easy to read. The best ones are pie charts, bar/column charts and line charts. Don't go overboard with complicated charts, such as doughnut, bubble or radar charts.
- Don't spend too much time using a wide variety of unusual colours.
- Make sure your chart has a title/legend.

Once you have completed your charts or graphs, think about what your results mean and then try to explain and interpret the information. Often how you interpret your results will depend on the aim of your questionnaire and the questions you asked.

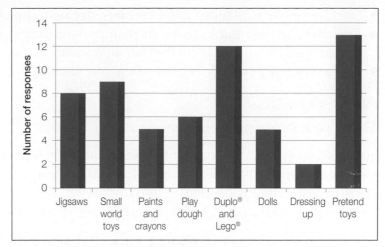

Chart showing popularity of different toys

It is OK to start with the obvious. For example:

The results of this question show that most parents send their children to nursery.

However, this will not get you very high marks for analysis, so try to think about *why* most parents send their children to nursery. For example:

Pie chart showing how many parents use nurseries

I think this might be because nowadays both parents often work either full-time or part-time and so need someone to look after their children. They might also want their children to play with lots of other children and going to a nursery also helps them get ready for school.

Once all the questions have been analysed, you need to evaluate the information you have collected and suggest how some of it might be used in the rest of your task. For example, your results might highlight some aspect of your research that parents want to know more about, or you might be able to use one of your charts in the actual outcome itself because you think it is important.

Evaluating secondary research

When you carry out secondary research, you need to find out the facts about the topic you have chosen. This will help you to understand the topic better. Any secondary research you carry out must be evaluated.

Try to evaluate the importance of the information you have selected.

- Start by briefly explaining what you were trying to find out and why.
- Explain what you think are the most important things you have learnt from your research and why you think they are important.
- Explain how this will be helpful when you plan the rest of your task.

Analysing visits

This is your on-going evaluation.

You need to evaluate every visit in your child study. In your evaluation, you have to look at all four areas of development (physical, intellectual, emotional and social) to see how your child is developing and improving. You also need to comment on how the activities you chose have helped encourage development.

You need to plan how to evaluate your visits. Using a chart is a good way to start:

1. Divide a sheet of A4 paper into boxes. Look at the two examples below and choose whichever one you think is best for you.

Physical	Intellectual
Emotional	Social

Example 1

Physical	Intellectual
Fine motor skills	Cognitive skills
Gross motor skills	Language
Sensory skills	
Emotional	Social
Positive	Behaviour
Negative	Social skills

Example 2

2. Read through your notes from the visit.

3. Use different, coloured pens to highlight or underline examples of the different types of development you noticed during the visit. Make brief notes on these in the appropriate boxes. Don't worry if you have more in one box than another, but try to write something in every box.

4. Now think about what your child can do and compare it to what an average child of that age is able to do.

5. Try to find one or two quotes you could use to support your opinions.

6. Now you should be able to write one or two paragraphs for each area of development.

7. Finally, you need to think about the activities you did with the child and the types of development they encouraged. You need to write a short paragraph about this. Don't worry if you say that something went wrong or the child did not enjoy it. You can still gain marks by saying things were not successful, as long as you say why and what you might change for the next time.

 **Think about**

> Were the activities you did with the child useful? What skills and types of development did they encourage? Did the child enjoy them? Were they suitable for the age of the child? What might you change?

Final evaluation of child study

This is the last section of the child study.

You need to use the final evaluation to:

- show how your child has progressed since the start of the study
- decide how your child compares to the expected stage of development for a child of the same age
- evaluate how successful your research and the activities you chose for the visits have been in helping you to observe development and helping the child to develop different skills.

Presentation and the final outcome for the research task

For the final outcome for the research task, you are given different ideas to choose from, as shown below.

Possible ideas for outcomes:

Leaflet

Fact sheet

Booklet

Information pack

PowerPoint

No matter which you choose, you need to plan very carefully what you are going to include and how you will present the information. This is a great chance to show off your presentation skills and to improve your marks. For the final outcome, you *can* use different fonts, colours, backgrounds and illustrations.

PowerPoint presentations

 Remember

A PowerPoint presentation is used to give information to a group of people (e.g. at an antenatal class).

Guidelines

- **Keep it simple – not too much information on each slide. The person presenting will give the detail.**
- **Use pictures and illustrations – they can often say more than words.**
- **Don't make the presentation too long – people get bored.**
- **Use the right font and size so it's easy to read.**
- **Choose colours for background and font carefully.**

 top tips

1. Select the most important information from your research – do not simply cut and paste everything.

2. If you have time (or you want to), you can add presenter notes to the slides. These highlight the extra information to be given. The presenter can see them but not the people watching.

3. Why not produce a handout to go with your presentation?

Leaflets, booklets and fact sheets

Leaflets and fact sheets tend to be only one sheet of paper but you can make them more individual and interesting by folding them in different ways, and of course you can use both sides.

Booklets tend to give more information so you can include more pages.

 top tips

1. Why not make the outcomes different and more eye-catching by using different shapes and styles – the examples below might give you some ideas.

2. Find a leaflet – it does not have to be about child development – and analyse it to help you decide what makes a good leaflet design.

3. You can find examples of leaflets on the internet.

Leaflets and booklets need to be clear and colourful with appropriate illustrations

Information packs

These usually contain a mixture of booklets, fact sheets, leaflets and vouchers, but they can also include quizzes and games.

 Remember

You don't have to make everything that might go into an information pack!

References and plagiarism

Referencing

In both of your controlled assessments, you will need to use different secondary sources, such as books, websites, leaflets, videos and magazines, to find information to help you understand more about the topics you have chosen. You should also try to use quotes and references to support your own ideas and opinions, especially in your child study – this will help to improve your marks.

Whenever you use information from any of these sources, you *must* say where the information is from. This is called referencing.

Plagiarism

When you copy someone else's work – from a book, a website or even another student – and present it as your own, this is known as plagiarism and is actually a form of stealing!

So whenever you use information from other people's work for your secondary research, you must reference it (say where you got the information).

> **! Remember**
>
> When you hand in your final piece of work, you have to sign a form saying that the work is your own. If it is not (and teachers and examiners will be able to recognise copied work, especially from textbooks), it could mean that your work is disqualified, so do not take the risk!

How to reference

There are several different ways of referencing – it does not matter which one you use, as long as you do it!

When researching background information

Copying out large chunks of information is not a good idea and will not help you to gain high marks, unless you analyse and evaluate it carefully (see page 19). However, if you do this, you should put the information in quotation marks and give the author's name. For example, see the box on the next page.

Why children have accidents

'The risk, frequency and place of accidents, as well as the type of accident depends on the child's age and stage of development.

Babies and young children have more accidents at home as this is where they spend most of their time. As they develop new skills and become more mobile the risk of accidents increases and, as they become older, they become more adventurous and curious so the type of accident likely to happen changes. Because they lack experience they have no real understanding of danger so for them something like water is fun because they play with it in the bath.'

(*AQA Child Development For GCSE*, Brennand and Hall, page 36)

 top tip

> Don't copy lots of information. Try to put it into your own words, and then analyse and evaluate it (see page 19).

When using quotes to support your own ideas

Daisy chose a pink piece of shiny paper to start her collage – *Child Development Controlled Assessment Guide* by Valerie Hall and Heather Brennand says that 'handling different materials will help to develop sensory skills'.

Daisy chose a pink piece of shiny paper to start her collage – from my research, I know that handling different materials can help to develop sensory skills (Hall and Brennand, 2004).

Information from the internet

If you take information from the internet, you must name the main web page you used.

For example, if you wanted to find some information about garden safety, you might use the 'Safe Kids' website. If you use any of the information you find, you should state the main website in brackets at the point you have used it.

Although nearly half of the accidents that happen in a garden involve adults 'almost a quarter involve children and 14% infants and toddlers' (www.safekids.co.uk).

Bibliography

At the end of your work, you need to include a bibliography – a list of all the sources you have used. Books should be listed by author, date, title and publisher. For example:

Hall, V. and Brennand, H. (2004) *Child Development: Coursework Guide for GCSE*, London: Hodder Arnold.

If you have used websites, you should give the full website address. For example:

http://www.safekids.co.uk/GardenSafetyAndChildren.html

If you have used magazines, leaflets, booklets, DVDs or TV programmes, you should name the title and the author/publisher if known.

Step-by-step guide to the research task

3

This section looks in more detail at what needs to be included in your research task. It gives you ideas, tips and techniques that will help you to plan and organise your work.

The research task is the shorter of the two controlled assessment tasks you have to do. It is worth 20 per cent of the final grade and is marked out of 30.

The tasks are based on the following areas:

- parenthood
- pregnancy
- diet, health and care of the child
- support for the parent and child.

You will probably do your research task some time during the first year of the course when you are being taught the relevant section of work – that way your teacher can help and support you. It is also a good way to learn information that will help you in your exam!

You only have to submit one research task. However, your teacher might organise with you to do two or three – that way you can choose the one that was best.

What are the tasks?

The tasks are set by AQA and there are two to choose from for each of the four areas. No matter which one you choose, you will need to show your skills of planning, research, analysis, evaluation and presentation.

So, where do you start? What follows will give you an idea of what you need to do, but your teacher will support and guide you as you do the work.

The first thing to do is choose a task – your teacher will be on hand to help you with this. Once you have done this, there are seven main steps to completing the task.

This gives you an outline of what you need to do and the skills you need to use. Use the Unit 2 research task chart in the Appendix to help you keep on track (see page 131).

Step 1: What do I actually have to do for this task? (Analysing the task)

Start by writing out the task you have chosen (the examiner needs to know what you are doing).

What is the actual purpose and main focus for the task? Think about what sort of information you might need to find out about, why it is important and what you are going to use it for. What do you have to do with the information?

Don't just re-write the task using exactly the same words – show that you really understand why this topic is important. This should not take more than one or two paragraphs but you need to do this to make your planning easier.

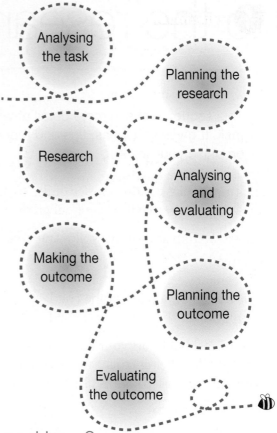

Step 2: What am I going to do and how? (Planning the research)

Once you have analysed the task, you should have some idea of what sort of information you will need to find out about (research).

 **top tip**

> Don't worry too much about what your final outcome will be. You cannot decide on this until you have done your research.

Stage A

Start by working in rough and thinking about the following questions:

- What sort of information will you need to find out?
- Why do you think it is important?

- Where will you get the information?
- Will you use primary or secondary research, and for what?
- How will you write up and present the information?

 **Remember**

Keep all of your ideas in your work folder.

Now, think again!

Although you will be able to do some research out of school or as homework, you only have a limited amount of time to organise and write up your research, so be realistic! While you need to try to include both primary and secondary research, will you really have time to do interviews and questionnaires as well as a survey and a visit? Think about what will give you the best information.

Stage B

For Stage B, you need to look at your notes and make a rough draft of your action plan.

Check through it and then write it up. It is up to you how you present it. You could:

- use a flow chart
- use a mind map
- use a table or chart
- simply write it out.

However, use only **one** of these types of presentation.

 **top tips**

You can increase your chances of gaining good marks by writing a good planning section. Just make sure you include what information you want to find, whether it is primary or secondary, why it is important and how you will present it.

 **Remember**

You can always change your plan – just explain how and why.

Step 3: Finding and organising information (Research)

In some ways, this is the easy bit, especially if you have done your planning carefully.

Stage A

Carry out your primary and secondary research and keep all your work in your class folder.

Stage B

Sort, organise and present all your information.

top tip

> You should not include every piece of research, especially those from books and websites. You can improve your marks by being concise and selective.

Each piece of research should include the following:

- a sentence explaining what you were trying to find out and why
- a description of the research itself
- references to show where you got the information (see page 26).

Step 4: What have I found out and how useful might it be in planning my outcome? (Analysing and evaluating)

This is a very important section but it is not difficult.

Look back at what you have written and planned for Steps 1 and 2. Think about what your outcome has to be about.

Stage A

Read through each piece of research, then pick out what you think is the most important information and explain why. This is **analysis**. Now summarise and write this up at the end of that piece of research.

Remember

> You need to concentrate on the information you have used, not on how easy or difficult it was to find, etc.

Stage B

After you have analysed all your research, think about which might be the most useful pieces of information and what you might include in a final outcome.

You may have found out a lot of new and useful information in your research but you will not be able (and should not) use all of it when planning and making your outcome. You need to summarise the information and think about what might be the most useful to include in your outcome and give reasons why. This is your **evaluation**.

By now, you should be ready to decide what your outcome will be about and start planning it.

Step 5: What will my outcome be and how will I do it? (Planning the outcome)

You are getting near to the end now! This step should not take you long to do.

You need to decide:

- what the main purpose of your outcome will be and why
- what sort of outcome you might make (e.g. a leaflet, booklet or PowerPoint presentation), and why (see page 24)
- who the outcome is for

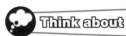

Think about

Try to think about a 'target group'. Is it for new parents, parents, expectant mums, older mums, teenagers? This could help you decide what information to include.

- what information you will include and why

Remember

Plan this very carefully and make sure you show how you are going to use your research. You don't have to include all your research, just what *you* think is important. Being selective will help you gain marks – just cutting and pasting will not.

- how you will present your information – make it colourful and easy to read and try to include different types of presentation.

top tip

Why not analyse a leaflet, booklet or poster to decide what makes a good one? Think about colour, layout, font size, illustrations, etc. (see page 23).

A good planning section will gain you more marks, and it does not have to be a big piece of work. You could present much of the detail in a chart (see below).

What I will include	Why	How I will present it and why

The main topics you will research, not all the detail

How and why this research might be useful

Ideas about using charts, lists, bullet points, ICT, pictures, etc.

Finally in this section, think about the layout – what you will include on each page and section. Think about the size and shape and what you learnt from your leaflet analysis. Then simply sketch one or more ideas. Choose which one you think is best and give some more detail (see below).

Remember

In your sketch, do not include all the information you are going to put into the final outcome. Just give a brief idea of what will go where.

You could list the materials you will need to make your outcome.

Sketch of a possible layout for a leaflet

top tip

Think about how much time you have – do not try to do too much!

Step 6: Making the outcome

Just do it!

Step 7: How good is it? (Evaluating the outcome)

This is the last step to success!

This should be mainly about how successful you think your finished outcome is. However, you should also try to comment on how good your planning and research were and/or what you think you might have done better. What you should not do is evaluate all your research again. You have already done that.

Look through all the different steps for doing your research task and think about the following:

- How successful was your outcome? Look at the original task and your analysis – does it answer what you were asked to do?
- Look at your planning for your outcome. Is what you have made suitable for your target group and does it give them the information they might need? What about what your outcome looks like? Is it colourful and easy to read? Does it contain the right information?
- Did you have to make any changes, especially when making your outcome? Explain why (this can actually help you gain marks).
- What do other people think of your outcome, especially people from your target group?

 **top tip**

Plan a quick and simple survey to get other people's views. Make a checklist of points for them to look at (see page 10). Show them your outcome and ask them to fill in their answers. They could even give you a rating out of ten. Give a brief analysis of the results. This would also be an easy way to include another piece of primary research to help improve your marks.

Step-by-step guide to the child study

This section looks in more detail at what needs to be included in the child study. It will give you ideas, examples, tips and techniques to help you plan and organise your work.

The child study is the longer of the two controlled assessment tasks you have to do. It is worth 40 per cent of the final grade and is marked out of 60.

In your child study, you need to show your knowledge and understanding of how children develop and learn. This task is based mainly on the 'Development of the child' section of the specification.

As part of this piece of work, you have to choose one controlled assessment task to work on. These have been set by AQA and there are six to choose from.

You will probably carry out the child study in the second year of the course. As with the research task, your teacher will support and guide you through each stage and make sure you have learnt the skills you need for this piece of work.

Once you have chosen a child to study, there are seven main steps to completing the task, as shown below.

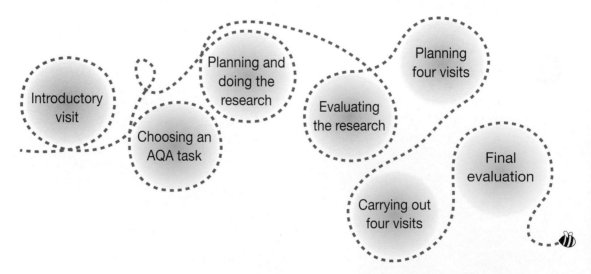

Introductory visit

Choosing an AQA task

Planning and doing the research

Evaluating the research

Planning four visits

Carrying out four visits

Final evaluation

So, where do you start?

Choosing a child to study

The first thing you need to do is choose a child to study. You will need to ask the parents' permission because you will need to have regular contact with them, the child and possibly other members of the family over quite a long period of time.

 Remember

> The exam specification states that you must study a child who will be under the age of five years by the end of the study.

Consider the following:

- If possible, try to avoid studying a newborn or very young baby. Young babies tend to spend a lot of time sleeping and development can be difficult to notice.
- Choosing an older child can also be difficult. As the child gets nearer to the age of five, their development begins to even out, especially their physical development, so you may not see as much change and progression.
- Studying younger brothers and sisters may also be difficult. Because you probably see them very often, you may not find it as easy to spot how and when their development changes.

 Think about

> The aim of the study is to show how much you know and understand about how children learn and develop new skills. Choosing to study a child with a disability, especially a severe disability, may make this difficult.

 Remember

> Whoever you choose to study, you must make sure that no one will be able to recognise or identify the child or the child's family. You can use the child's first name, as well as other family first names, but do not include:
> → surnames
> → addresses or telephone numbers
> → maps showing the area or highlighting the child's home
> → copies of letters with names or addresses.

Once you have the parents' permission, you are ready to start your study.

Step 1: Introductory visit

This is the start of your study – it is the first visit. The aim of this visit is to find out as much as you can about exactly what your child can do.

top tip

When writing up your introduction, use the suggested headings in this section. This will help you to organise your information and it will be easier to check you have included everything.

Remember

→ Give your own opinions about how you think your child's development compares with the milestones expected for their age.
→ Try to use specialist terms as well as quotes and references to support your opinions.

You need to write a fairly detailed description of the child so that the person reading it has a clear picture of the child.

Do not expect to be able to get all the information you need at one visit – you might have to make two or three short visits close together. You might also need to ask the parents questions about something that you have not been able to see the child do, but try to rely on your own observations.

Remember

Unless you are studying a newborn baby, do not give detailed background information about where the child was born, or when they got their first tooth, made their first steps or said their first word. If it is not relevant, do not include it – you will not get extra marks.

You need to include all of the following in your introduction:

- physical description
- personality
- family background
- home and local area
- physical development
- intellectual development
- emotional development
- social development
- play.

Physical description

Give the date of birth and age of the child at the beginning of your study – in years and months, or months and weeks. Think about what the child looks like and describe this. You could include information on:

- height and weight
- shape of face, nose and mouth
- eye colour and shape
- any freckles or dimples
- build – slim, tall, plump, sturdy
- skin tone and colour

Personality

How would you describe the child's personality – what sort of a child are they?

Are they:

- happy
- loving
- outgoing
- quiet
- mischievous
- reserved
- shy
- timid
- easily bored
- excitable
- friendly
- temperamental?

Try to say how the child shows their personality.

Family background

Include any *relevant* information about the child's family. For example, is the child an only child, the youngest, the oldest, the middle child, the only boy, the only girl? Think about and write up how this might affect the child's behaviour and development, and explain why.

You should also consider the following:

- What type of family does the child belong to?
- Is it a nuclear, one-parent, step/reconstituted, large or extended family?
- Do the parents work? If so, who looks after the child?
- Does the child go to a nursery or a childminder?
- Do the family spend quality time together? If so, when and where?

Again, try to explain how this might affect the child's development and learning.

Home and local area

Briefly describe the child's home.

- Does the child have his/her own bedroom or do they share?
- Is there somewhere for them to play, both inside and outdoors?
- What about safety in the home?
- Do they have lots of toys, books and games? What sort? How would these help development?

Briefly describe the area the child lives in.

- Is it a small village, a town, in the middle of a city?
- Are there parks, playgroups and nurseries nearby?

 **Remember**

> Keep asking yourself 'How might this affect development?'.

Physical development

Gross motor skills

You can see these when a child uses the large muscles in their arms and legs to walk, run, throw, etc.

So, can your child:

- crawl
- cruise
- walk
- climb
- hop
- skip
- walk on tiptoe

- jump
- balance
- climb stairs
- kick a ball
- catch a ball
- pick up large objects
- ride a tricycle?

You need to describe how you know they can do these things. Try to encourage the child to do some simple tasks and watch carefully. For example, *'I asked Joe to show me his bedroom. As we walked upstairs, I noticed that he went up with one foot on each step but came back down with two feet on each step.'*

 Think about

> Don't simply list things the textbook says a child of that age can do, and then say they can! You need to show how you *know* they can do these things – this is evidence that you have observed the child.

Fine motor skills

You can see these when a child is doing things with their hands and fingers, using their smaller muscles.

So, can your child:

- pick up small things
- put things down carefully
- hold objects
- turn knobs
- fasten buttons and zips

- build with bricks
- hold a pencil or crayon
- draw
- thread beads
- do a jigsaw?

Again, describe how you know they can do these things. Try to include specialist terms (e.g. pincer grasp, tripod grasp).

 top tip

> You could use a checklist, but you must make sure that you describe exactly what you have seen the child doing as evidence.

Sensory development

All children use their senses to explore and learn. These are:

- sight
- touch
- hearing
- taste
- smell.

Babies explore everything with their mouths (mouthing) but all children need to have the chance to use their senses to explore their surroundings.

What toys and games does the child have that would help them to do this?

Intellectual development

Language skills

Babies begin to learn how to communicate with other people at birth, through eye contact, pointing, listening, making sounds and copying others. This is called non-verbal communication.

From about one year, they might begin to use simple words or sign language. This is called verbal communication.

- How well can your child talk and communicate?
- Do they use sounds, single words, short phrases or complete sentences? Try to give examples.
- Do they use their hands to help them communicate (e.g. pointing)?
- Can they understand more words than they can use? Give examples.
- What sort of words do they know – family names, household objects, toys, etc.?
- How do the parents encourage language development?
- Do they know simple songs or nursery rhymes? Which ones?
- Do they have speech difficulties? Give examples.

 top tip

> If you write down words or phrases the child is using now, at the end of your study you will be able to compare how they talk then with how they talked at the start of the study. This way you will be able to highlight how they have improved.

Cognitive development

Cognitive development is all about how children develop their thinking, reasoning and learning skills – understanding numbers and concepts, reading, writing and drawing are all part of cognitive development. It also involves memory, concentration and problem solving etc.

Describe what the child knows and understands. Do they understand anything about:

- colour
- size and shape
- numbers and letters
- time
- past, present, future
- opposites (e.g. big and little)
- cause and effect
- object permanence
- weight
- floating and sinking?

Emotional development

Emotional development is about feelings – how the child feels about themselves and about others and how they show their feelings. For example, if they are happy, what do they do? If they are angry, how do they show it?

Feelings and emotions can be both positive and negative.

Positive emotions	Negative emotions
• Love	• Jealousy
• Happiness	• Fear
• Excitement	• Anger
• Pleasure	• Frustration
• Joy	• Sadness
• Pride	• Loneliness
• Confidence	• Anxiety

Try to find out if your child has a comforter – for example, a blanket, toy, dummy or their thumb. When and why do they need one?

Social development

Children have to learn certain social skills so that they can make friends, play and get on with other people. To do this, they have to know how to behave and act around other people in a variety of different social situations.

Try to find out and write about the child's behaviour.

- How does the child behave?
- Do they say 'please' and 'thank you'?
- Will they share and take turns when playing?
- How do they behave when they meet family, other children, strangers, adults?
- Do they have temper tantrums – when?

Also, find out and write about the child's social skills.

- Does the child have the chance to meet other adults and children (e.g. at playgroup, the nursery, the park)?
- Does the child have any special friends?
- Can they go to the toilet by themselves?
- Can they wash and dry their hands and face, clean their teeth, get dressed?
- Can they feed themselves?

Play

Try to find out what sort of toys your child has and what they enjoy playing with. Look at what kind of play they enjoy. For example, do they enjoy imaginative play or do they prefer playing outdoors? Do they mostly play on their own or can they play happily with other children? This will help you to choose a topic for the next stage of the study.

Have you used quotes, references and specialist terms?

Conclusion

This is the first bit of evaluation – it should not be a huge piece of work, so don't re-write everything you have already written!

This should just be a summary, about one paragraph, of how well *you* think they are doing and what you have learnt about them.

The conclusion is important because you need to use it to help you to choose a suitable AQA child study task to research as the next part of the study.

The better your introduction, the easier it will be to plan your visits and do your final evaluation.

Step 2: Choosing an AQA task

Your teacher will give you a list of tasks to choose from.

Look at the list and think about what you know about your child. From your introduction you should have a good idea of the stage of development your child has reached, what they like to do, what sorts of toys and games they have and what sort of play they enjoy.

Choose a research topic that you think is the most suitable for the age and stage of development of the child, and one that you think you and they will enjoy.

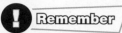

Remember

What you choose should help your child's development and be something you can research easily.

Step 3: Planning and doing the research

Stage A

Write out the task you have chosen. Write a paragraph to explain why you think this is the best task to choose and how it will help the child's development and learning.

Stage B

Before you start your research, you must plan what you need to do and think about why it is important. You only have a limited amount of time to carry out and write up your research.

Remember

The research has to help you in planning some activities to do with your child in two of your visits.

Start by making rough notes and thinking about the following:

- What sort of information will you need to find out?
- How will it help you to plan the visits?
- Where will you get the information?
- Will you use primary or secondary research, and for what?
- How will you write up and present the information?

Remember

Keep all of your ideas in your work folder.

Now write up your ideas. A good planning section will help you gain more marks, and it does not have to be a big piece of work. As in the research task, you could present much of the detail about what you will include in a chart (see below).

What I will include	Why	How I will present it and why

The main topics you will research, not all the detail

How and why this research might be useful

Ideas about using charts, lists, bullet points, ICT, pictures, etc.

top tip

Check! Have you planned to do some primary as well as secondary research?

Stage C

Now, do all your research! Try to include both primary and secondary research and make sure you keep all your information, notes and ideas at school in your folder.

Then select, sort, organise and present all your information.

top tip

You should not include every piece of research, especially those from books and websites. You can improve your marks by being concise and selective.

Think about

Try to use different methods of presentation.

Each piece of research should include the following:
- a sentence explaining what you were trying to find out and why
- the research itself
- references to show where you got the information (see page 26).

Choose what you are going to include very carefully. You need to make sure that you:

- link your information to the age and stage of development of your child and to what you know they can do and will enjoy
- include information and ideas for activities.

Step 4: Evaluating the research – what is important and how might I use it?

You must use your research to help plan activities for two of your visits.

As in your research task, you need to briefly analyse and evaluate the research you have done.

- Start by briefly explaining what you were trying to do in your research.
- Briefly explain how and why you did your research.
- Write about what you have learnt from it that you think is important.
- Explain how your research will be helpful in planning activities for two of your visits.

Step 5: Planning four visits

You need to plan and carry out four visits over a period of four months. In these visits, you need to plan some activities that will help you to look at the physical, intellectual, emotional and social development of your child.

In **two** of the visits, the activities should be based on your research task. For the other two visits, you can choose any other activities you think the child will enjoy. These do not have to be based on the research task.

Use a **simple** planning chart for your visits. You don't have to give details of your planning for the visits at this stage! However, it would be a good idea if you could show which two areas of development you think your activities might encourage the most.

 **Remember**

> You should never be in charge of the child on your own. If you plan any outdoor activities, check with the parents – they should always be present on these visits.

Visit	Dates	Activities	Link to task	PIES
1	Oct.	• Reading a book • Dressing up		P + I
2	Nov.	• Playing in garden	✓	P + E
3	Dec.	• Sand and water play	✓	P + I
4	Jan.	• Painting		P + S

Aims and planning

An aim explains what you want to find out during the visits.

For example:

In this visit I am going to make and decorate some small cakes with James. I think this will help his physical development, especially his fine motor skills and sensory development, as well as his understanding of concepts such as size and numbers.

Planning is all about being organised and prepared. Good planning will help your visits go well and help you to get the information you want so that you can see how the child is developing.

Planning – extra research (where needed)

As part of your planning, you should try to find out some extra information about your chosen activities that you think will:

- help your visits go well
- help you decide on appropriate expectations.

 **Remember**

> This research needs to be no more than one or two pages.

For the two visits based on the externally set task, most of your research should already have been done. Don't write it all out again! You should refer back to this to show how you are using it. You may, however, also decide to do some extra research directly related to the chosen activities (e.g. a risk assessment if going to the park or if making cakes, thinking about what to make).

For the other two visits, you might include some, but not all, of the following as part of your planning:

- A short interview with the parents – no more than two or three questions. This could be a simple telephone interview.
- Looking at the ingredients/materials/methods for the activity and saying how they could be adapted for your child.
- A risk assessment for the activity or area where the activity will take place.
- An inventory of the child's toys or equipment to find out what they have that you could use.
- Checking in textbooks to see how the activity could help to promote all areas of development. You could use a spidergram for this.
- Different activities within the main activity. For example, if painting, what sort of painting would be best for the child and why?

Keep the additional research brief and relevant.

Expectations/predictions

These describe what you think will happen and what development the child might show when doing your planned activities.

Try to give reasons why. These could be based on:

- what you know about the child
- what you know about average development for the age of your child.

Try to give some references from appropriate textbooks. For example:

Socially I expect that he will be able to play happily alongside Steven because, according to Brennand et al., a child of two should "begin to enjoy parallel play".

Try to give several expectations for each of the areas of development you are looking at.

Don't simply copy out a long list of milestones as your expectations!

Step 6: Carrying out four visits

This is the fun bit – this is where you can enjoy playing with the child and learning about their development. But do not forget to make some notes as soon as you can after the visit!

 Remember

> You will have to write up your visits in school under supervision so your notes will be very important.

In your notes, comment on:

- what the child did
- whether the child enjoyed the activities
- how the child reacted
- whether the activities were successful.

The visit starts when you arrive and ends when you leave, so try to record everything that happens, otherwise you could miss a lot of interesting details that might help you understand other areas of development.

 top tip

> Taking photographs of the activity could help you remember what happened.

Observations (writing up the visit)

If your notes are good, this should be easy.

top tip

> When you write up your observations, record everything that happened during the visit, not just the activity, because you need to look at all four areas of development.

Make sure you write your visits up with as much detail as possible. This will make it easier for you to do your evaluation.

If you have taken photographs of the child during the visits they can be used in your write-up, but you must refer to them to show development and the skills the child is using.

What about your planning? Did you have everything you needed? Did you have to change anything? If so why?

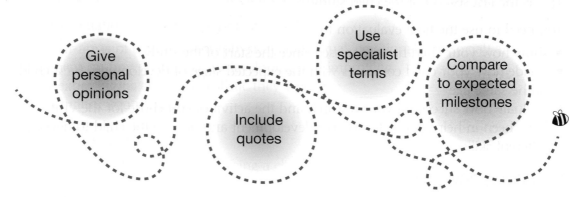

Give personal opinions

Include quotes

Use specialist terms

Compare to expected milestones

Bibliography and appendix

Finally, list all the books, magazines, websites, computer software, etc. that you have used in the bibliography. Include any research materials that you have used (e.g. leaflets and examples of child's work) in the appendix.

Practical activities

In this section, we will look at ideas for activities that could be planned for your child study visits and how they might help physical, intellectual, emotional and social development.

Play is something that children do instinctively – they learn by playing and, during any one day, they will enjoy lots of different types of play. Many of these types of play are the same but with different names.

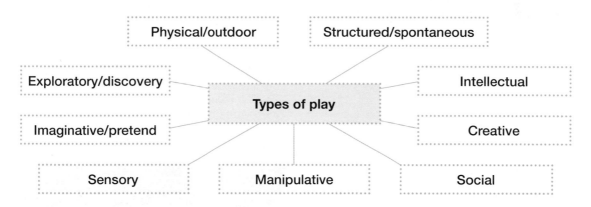

There are four main types of play:
- creative play
- imaginative or pretend play
- physical play
- manipulative play.

How play can help children's development

These four main types of play are often associated with particular activities and particular skills. However, it must be remembered that all the different types of play will allow children to use and develop a wide range and variety of skills, covering all aspects of development.

Dressing up, for instance, is a form of imaginative play that allows children to take on different roles and act out their ideas and feelings. But it will also help social and emotional development, language development, and often physical development, including fine motor and gross motor skills, and sensory development.

Creative play

Creative play takes place when children use different materials to make something by using their own ideas and imagination.

Creative play lets them explore and experiment with different materials, use their senses and express their own ideas and feelings about the world they live in. It also helps their fine motor skills.

The end result may not be recognisable and the child may not even want to keep it! It is important, however, that what they make is praised and not made fun of.

How creative play can help learning and development

Physical development

- Using crayons, pens, brushes, scissors, and so on can help develop fine motor skills, hand–eye coordination and handling and control.
- Painting at an easel or doing foot/hand prints can help gross motor skills.
- Creative activities help to develop sensory skills, especially sight and touch.

Intellectual – concepts

- Using colours, textures, shapes and space will help to develop creativity.
- Creative activities such as painting, making collages and modelling will help develop imagination.
- All of these activities can help to develop concentration and memory.
- Painting and making models will help to develop problem-solving skills.
- Helps children learn about different materials and properties.
- Helps to develop an understanding of different concepts.

Intellectual – language

- Children will enjoy talking about what they have made.
- They will learn new words.
- They will be encouraged to ask questions, listen and follow instructions.

Emotional development

- All these activities allow children to experience both positive and negative emotions, e.g. pride, excitement, frustration, happiness.
- They can increase children's confidence and self-esteem.
- They encourage independence.
- They allow children to make choices.
- Children can express feelings without using words.
- Prevents boredom.
- Gets rid of tension – helps children 'let off steam'.

Social development

Children will learn to:
- share
- cooperate and take turns
- accept and follow rules ad instructions.

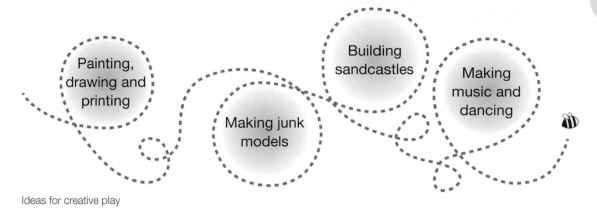

Ideas for creative play

Imaginative play

Imaginative play is sometimes known as pretend play. It takes place when children act out being somebody or something else – for example, mum or dad, a robot, a tiger, a pop star.

Children learn by copying and imitating what they see and hear, and so often in this sort of play they use real-life situations that they may have seen, heard or experienced, and may pretend to be someone else. This is called role play.

Role play is important for children because it lets them use their imaginations to act out their own feelings and emotions, and it also gives them a chance to experience other people's feelings when they take on different roles.

For imaginative play, children may dress up for their part and use toys and everyday objects as 'props' in the story. For example, a cardboard box may become a train, a space ship or a boat; their soft toys and teddies become the people in their stories.

Up to 18 months	Children will 'imitate' and copy adult actions, e.g. waving goodbye, playing peek-a-boo.
18 months–2 years	Simple pretend play will start, usually involving favourite toys and dolls. Children will act out everyday situations, e.g. getting dressed, having tea, going to bed, shopping.
2–2½ years	Children will take on other roles that they know, such as mum and dad. Then they will begin to include ideas from characters in books, stories and TV programmes that they have seen or heard but not experienced. This is often called fantasy play.
2½–3 years onwards	Children will enjoy imaginative play together and will start to negotiate roles.

Stages of imaginative play

How imaginative play can help learning and development

Physical development
- Develops fine and gross motor skills when dressing up or making props for role play.
- Small world play will develop fine motor skills and hand–eye coordination.
- Imaginative play outdoors can develop gross motor skills, balance and coordination.
- Develops spatial awareness.

Intellectual – concepts
- Helps to develop imagination and creativity when planning and making up stories and plays.
- Small world play helps to develop understanding of the world and how things work.
- Helps children to understand the concept of past, present and future.
- May help to develop maths and numeracy skills.
- Allows children to explore and experiment.
- Problem solving.

Emotional development
Helps children to:
- experience and act out feelings, e.g. sadness, enjoyment, frustration, anger, happiness
- share and act out feelings that may be difficult to express
- release tension and stress
- build confidence and self-esteem
- understand how other people feel
- work through new or problem situations, e.g. moving house, going to the doctor/dentist, the arrival of a new baby.

Intellectual – language
Children will:
- learn new words
- talk to themselves as they make up and act out stories
- listen to and talk to other people as they play together
- instruct others how to act out a certain role
- re-tell known stories with small world play
- tell own stories with small world play.

Social development
When playing with other children, it encourages:
- taking turns
- sharing
- cooperation
- negotiating about roles, space, equipment
- caring for others
- respect for other people's ideas and feelings
- solving problems together
- making friends.

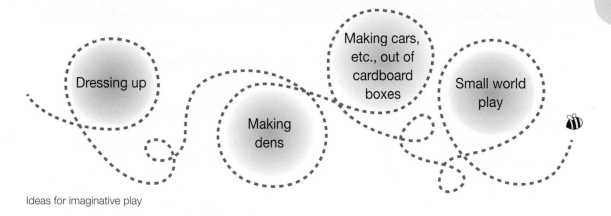

Ideas for imaginative play

Imaginary play does not require expensive toys and often needs little real planning because it depends on the child or children using their own ideas, imaginations and experiences. Parents and carers can only suggest ideas and then let the child develop them – if they want to!

What is most important is to have lots of things available for the child to use in this sort of play that will 'fire' their imaginations. For example:

- a box of old clothes or lengths of fabric
- accessories such as bags, hats, shoes or jewellery
- small world play toys
- cardboard boxes
- sheets and old curtains
- empty food packets, sweet and biscuit tins, boxes.

Then let the child's imagination take over.

Physical play

Most toys, games and activities will involve some sort of physical movement, and will help, in different ways, to develop physical skills. Many children's toys, games and activities tend to be done indoors and often concentrate on using fine motor skills.

As children grow, and become more mobile and curious, they need the chance to explore and investigate the world they live in, and they usually have lots of energy, which most indoor activities will not use up. They need to exercise and develop the larger body muscles in their arms and legs by running, jumping, climbing and skipping. To do this, they need to have lots of outdoor play, with space to run around so they can 'let off steam'.

This sort of play is also important because it gives children a chance to meet, play and mix with other children and people of different ages and cultures, which is an important part of their social development. It encourages sharing, taking turns and learning to cooperate.

Outdoor play is also important because it gives children a chance to explore different environments.

How physical play can help learning and development

Physical development

Helps to:
- improve gross motor skills
- develop balance and coordination
- strengthen muscles and bones
- build up stamina
- improve appetite
- improve heart rate and blood circulation
- improve skin tone – rosy cheeks
- develop the senses.

Intellectual – language

Helps children to:
- learn new words
- improve communication skills.

Intellectual – concepts

Helps with:
- developing awareness of space (spatial awareness)
- learning about cause and effect
- problem solving
- understanding seasons of the year
- developing concepts such as speed.

Social development

Playing with other children encourages:
- taking turns
- sharing and cooperation
- negotiating about roles, space, equipment
- respect for other people's ideas and feelings
- solving problems together
- making friends.

Emotional development
- Releases tension and stress.
- Lets off steam.
- Encourages independence.
- Builds confidence and self-esteem.
- Encourages positive emotions.

Hide and seek and 'tig'

Garden play on slides, swings, etc.

Visits to a soft play area

Ball games

Ideas for physical play

Manipulative play

Manipulative play usually involves children building or fitting things together. It is important because it helps them to begin to be more confident and competent in using all the different tools and equipment needed in life.

Manipulative play involves children developing their fine motor skills and hand–eye coordination.

How manipulative play can help learning development

Physical development

Helps to develop:
- different grasps and grips
- hand muscles
- skilful use of fingers
- hand–eye coordination.

Social development

If playing with other children, it encourages:
- taking turns
- sharing
- cooperation
- perseverance.

Intellectual – concepts

- Helps to develop problem-solving skills if making models or building.
- Encourages logical thinking.
- Encourages decision-making.
- Helps children use imagination to develop ideas.

Helps to develop concepts such as:
- shape
- size
- volume
- spatial awareness.

Emotional development

Helps children to:
- succeed and cope with failure in a fun way
- build confidence and self-esteem.

Intellectual – language

- Encourages language development.
- Increases vocabulary.

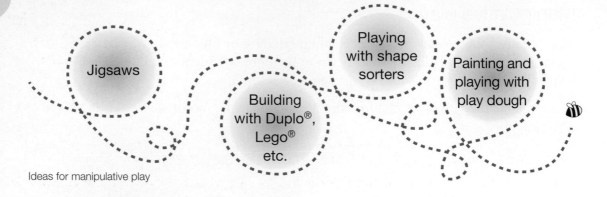

Ideas for manipulative play

When planning your visits, you need to think of different activities that the child will enjoy and that will also let you see different areas of development. You may have some ideas of your own but the following section may inspire you.

Painting, drawing and printing

As soon as young children can hold crayons in a palmar grasp, they will enjoy making marks on paper, even though these will not mean anything.

Painting, printing and drawing are great activities for children of all ages. They can help all areas of development and are great fun. If you plan a painting activity as part of your study or research, you will be able to find out a lot about the child's development, give the child a lot of pleasure by creating a 'work of art' (even though you might not be able to tell what it is!) and have lots of fun.

How painting, drawing and printing can help learning and development

Intellectual – concepts

- Using colours, textures, shapes and space will help to develop creativity.
- Painting, drawing and printing will help develop the imagination.
- Mixing colours together or adding sand or salt to change the texture helps children to understand cause and effect.
- All of these activities can help to develop concentration and memory.

Intellectual – language

- Children will enjoy talking about their drawings and paintings.
- They will be encouraged to ask questions, listen and follow instructions.
- They will learn new words about painting and drawing.

Physical development

- Using crayons, pens, brushes, etc. can help develop fine motor skills, hand–eye coordination and handling and control.
- Painting at an easel or doing foot/hand prints can help gross motor skills.
- All of these activities can develop sensory skills, especially sight and touch.

Emotional development

- All these activities allow children to experience both positive and negative emotions, e.g. pride, excitement, frustration, happiness.
- They can increase children's confidence and self-esteem.
- They encourage independence.
- They allow children to make choices and paint how they feel.

Social development

- Taking turns.
- Cooperating.
- Self control.
- Listening to instructions.

Other areas

- Numeracy – using and understanding numbers, sizes, shapes, repeats, patterns, sequences.
- Understanding of the world – looking at objects, flowers, animals, insects, using science and nature for ideas.

Planning

As with any activity, making the right choice and planning it carefully will make the experience more successful – both for the child and for you. Look at the different ideas shown below.

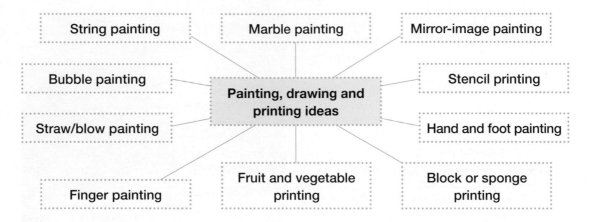

> ! **Remember**
>
> Before planning activities, check the following stages of drawing and make sure what you choose is suitable for the age of your child.

15 months	• May grasp a crayon using a palmar grasp. • Will use a crayon to scribble backwards and forwards.
18 months	• May hold a crayon with a primitive tripod grasp. • Beginning to show a preference for right or left hand.
2–2½ years	• Tries to hold a pencil close to the point in a primitive tripod grasp. • May make letters V and T. • Beginning to make circular scribbles and lift hand off paper to make lines.
3–3½ years	• Has quite good control of pencil between thumb and first two fingers. • Can draw circles, squares, lines, dots, etc. • Draws people, and a head with one or two features. • May talk about drawings before starting.
4–5 years	• Begins to add more details and uses more colours. • Drawings are more complex and varied. • Pictures will have more background. • Will draw houses with doors, windows, etc., trees, cars. • Can colour neatly.

Stages of drawing

Once you have chosen what you want to do, think about:

- what materials you will need and where to get them
- where you will do the activity
- covering the work surface or floor in case of accidents – newspapers or cheap plastic sheeting from a garden centre are good
- how you will dry paintings
- somewhere to wash and dry hands as you work
- wearing old clothes
- safety – using non-toxic paints, non–sharp equipment.

What about materials?

Materials for painting, drawing and printing can be expensive, but with a little thought and imagination you will probably be able to use things from around the home to produce exciting and different effects.

Paper	Old rolls of wallpaper or lining paper are excellent to use and are cheap. Old/used computer paper, backs of cards, insides of cereal boxes, backs of leaflets can all be used.
Paint	Powder paints are much easier to use than blocks of paint. You do not need lots of colours – choose primary colours, then you can experiment with mixing to create 'new' colours. Thick paint is best – you can add soap flakes to thicken it. Adding sand, salt or sugar to paint will change the texture.
Brushes	Short, fat brushes are best because they are easier to hold and control – one brush for each colour is best. Small house-painting brushes (2½ or 3½ cm) are good, as are old toothbrushes.
Things other than brushes	Be adventurous! Try using cotton buds, twigs or feathers. They will all make interesting and different marks.
Pots and palettes	You will need a pot for each colour of paint. Try to use containers that will not knock over easily, e.g. margarine tubs, yoghurt cartons, plastic egg boxes. Beware of jam jars – if knocked over, they can break.
Pens and crayons	Try to provide a variety of different types and thicknesses so the child can experiment – such as wax crayons, charcoal, plastic crayons, chalk, ordinary and coloured pencils. Even try felt tip pens, as long as they are non-toxic and impermanent.
Printing	Potatoes and turnips are good for cutting out shapes (you will need to do the cutting). You could also use fruit and vegetables, such as celery, carrots, leeks, apples, peppers. If this seems wasteful, look around at home and you will find lots you could use – cotton reels, thimbles, sponges, clothes pegs, balloons, corrugated paper, bubble wrap, pasta shapes, combs, biscuit cutters, and so on.

Materials for painting, drawing and printing

AQA HOME ECONOMICS FOR GCSE: CHILD DEVELOPMENT – CONTROLLED ASSESSMENT GUIDE

Painting and printing

 Remember

Children cannot always concentrate for a long time on one thing. Choose two or three different painting activities you think the child will enjoy and be able to do. Choosing something too difficult could end in tears and tantrums!

Finger/hand painting

You will need:

- powder paint
- wallpaper paste (non-fungicide)
- an easy-clean surface or large tray.

What to do

- Make up the paint with wallpaper paste to a thick consistency.
- Pour it onto a work surface or plastic tray.
- Let the child make patterns and shapes using their hands and fingers.

You could also:

- talk about the touch, feel and texture of the paint, introducing new words
- make hand prints onto paper.

Children enjoy finger and hand painting

Printing

You will need:

- saucer with different coloured paints
- potatoes
- paper.

What to do

- Cut the potato in half.
- Cut a different design onto each half.
- Dip the potato into the saucer of paint.
- Stamp onto a clean sheet of paper.

Printing is great for making patterns

You could also:

- rotate the print to make different patterns or use alternate colours
- use cut fruits and vegetables, bobbins, clothes pegs
- use sponges and experiment with thinner/thicker paints.

Blow painting

You will need:

- straws
- paper
- thin paint.

What to do

- Drizzle blobs of runny paint onto paper.
- Blow through straws in different directions to make patterns. Keep turning the paper round.
- Try using different colours.

Mirror-image painting

You will need:

- paper
- brushes
- coloured paint.

What to do

- Fold a piece of paper in half and open out.
- Use the brush to drop blobs of coloured paint onto one half.
- Fold over the other half of the paper again and smooth with your hand.
- Open out to see the pattern.

Blow painting creates weird and wonderful works of art

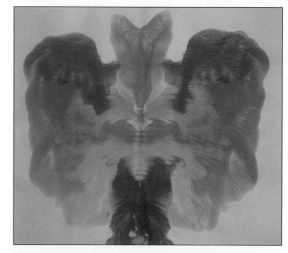

Mirror-image painting can show how colours change when mixed together

Bubble painting

You will need:

- mugs or small bowls
- paper
- paint
- washing-up liquid
- a straw.

What to do

- Put about 1 cm of water into a mug, cup or small bowl. Add a squeeze of paint and a squeeze of washing-up liquid.
- With a straw, blow to make lots of bubbles – enough so they start to go over the top of the mug or bowl.
- Carefully put a sheet of A4 paper over the top of the mug or bowl then lift off.
- You could use different colours and sizes on one sheet.

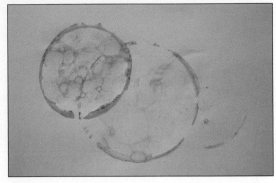

Bubble painting is great fun

Drawing

Drawing activities do not take as much organising as painting, and are usually not as messy, but they do need to be planned!

Drawing has to be learnt – and it takes time. How good children become will depend partly on whether they have natural ability and partly on whether they are given plenty of chances to practise and enjoy drawing.

Early 'drawings' will be just scribbles so do not expect anything you can recognise until the child is about three years old!

A three-year-old has good pencil control and can draw simple shapes

 Remember

→ Check out stages of drawing in textbooks and Chapter 6 (Development of the child) before planning.
→ Make sure pens, crayons and pencils are suitable for the age of the child. Big chunky crayons are easier for young children to handle.

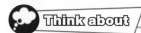

Think about

- Use bought colouring books – this will help to develop fine motor skills and hand–eye coordination. It takes a lot of skill to keep inside the lines.
- Make your own dot-to-dot drawings of familiar things – for example, flowers, balls, cars and houses.
- Draw around everyday objects, like stencils, wooden bricks, jigsaw puzzle pieces and even hands. You could then make faces or other objects out of them or colour them in.
- With older children, do simple drawings and get the child to colour them in.

Cutting and sticking

Cutting and sticking gives children lots of opportunities to be creative and to improve their fine motor skills and hand–eye coordination.

Cutting out paper and spreading glue is difficult for young children to do without some help until they are at least three years old, but they will enjoy tearing paper into strips and dropping it onto paper that you have already spread with glue (if they want to put pictures on, then you can cut them out). You could then sprinkle glitter or even flour over the page to hide the glue then shake it off over a sink.

A collage is a creative activity, where scraps of paper, fabric, photographs, string, twigs, leaves, foil, etc. are stuck onto a background. Like painting, drawing and printing, making a collage is a messy activity, which most children will enjoy. It is also an activity that will help all areas of development.

Collages can be quite simple and small, such as a birthday card, or they can be much larger and more detailed, such as a picture of a day at the beach or a farmyard scene. Making a collage may also involve painting and printing. Making collages can be quite difficult and take a lot of time, patience, concentration and skills.

How cutting and sticking can help learning and development

Physical development

Tearing, cutting and sticking will help children:
- develop gross motor skills – arm muscles
- develop and improve fine motor skills
- develop hand–eye coordination
- become skilful at using small hand-held tools.

Handling different materials will help to develop sensory skills.

Intellectual – concepts

These activities will help children:
- learn about and use new and different materials in different ways
- develop decision-making and problem-solving skills when deciding what to do and how to do it
- develop an understanding of concepts such as colour, size, shape, number etc.
- develop their imagination and creativity.

Intellectual – language

- Will improve and increase vocabulary – words for materials and tools, and descriptive words.
- Improve language skills by asking questions and following instructions.

Emotional development

These activities will help children:
- experience positive emotions – pride, contentment, enjoyment, happiness
- begin to learn to control frustration and anger
- develop patience and concentration
- develop their confidence and self-esteem.

Other areas

- Numeracy – sizes and shapes, making patterns, estimating amounts, counting, use of space.
- Art – learning to create and appreciate colour, shapes and textures.

Social development

- Learning to work with others.
- Sharing and cooperating.
- Communicating and following instructions.

Planning

If you try to do cutting and sticking with a young child, they will quickly become bored and very frustrated, so when planning these sorts of activities you must think about what skills your child has.

Cutting out is difficult. Children have to learn to use and coordinate their hand and finger movements in a totally new way – to snip. Once they have learnt to do this, they then have to plan where to cut and guide the scissors in the right direction. Even adults can have problems with this! Tearing paper into strips and shapes is just as exciting for young children and not as frustrating.

Gluing and sticking are also difficult – trying to put the glue where it is needed requires a lot of skill, as does positioning it onto the background in the right place.

So do not expect too much – even a five-year-old may not be able to cut out and glue accurately.

 Remember

> Make sure you choose something that is suitable for the age of the child and their stage of development.

2–2½ years	• Will enjoy tearing paper into strips. • May be able to cut thin, narrow paper with plastic scissors. • Can spread glue but will need help. • Can drop things onto a glued surface.
2½–3 years	• May be able to snip thin paper more confidently. • Can spread glue, if helped.
3½–4 years	• Can tear around pictures. • Can spread glue more carefully. • Can put glue onto the back of 'torn out' shapes and stick them down. • May begin to use scissors to cut out shapes.
4½–5 years	• Cutting skills are better but still not accurate. • May begin to arrange pictures.

Stages of cutting and sticking

You need to plan these activities carefully.

- Think about what you might make before you start! Have some ideas.
- With an older child (4–5 years), ask them what they would like to do.
- Decide where would be a suitable area to work and make sure tables and other surfaces are protected.
- Try to have somewhere nearby to wash hands.
- Have a good range of materials to work with, but do not put them all out at the start.
- Check you have everything you need.
- Do not 'take over' the activity and do everything for the child. The finished item does not have to be perfect!

! Remember

→ Make sure all glues, paints, etc. are non-toxic and washable.
→ Supervise all of the time.
→ Use blunt-ended scissors.

What about materials?

Paper and card	Tissue paper, coloured paper and card, newspaper, magazines, catalogues, leaflets, wallpaper, wrapping paper, crepe paper, birthday cards and Christmas cards.
Fabrics	Scraps of materials with different textures, e.g. wool, silk, satin, and leather. Knitting wools, embroidery threads, feathers, cotton wool balls and string.
Use with care	Sequins, glitter, sand, rice, dried beans, peas and pasta.
Natural materials	Leaves, stones, twigs, shells, corks, pieces of bark from trees, wood shavings, sand and flowers.
Glues	Glue sticks are good for gluing paper to paper or even lightweight fabrics to paper, but they can be hard to control.
	PVA glue is strong and will go transparent when it dries. You can use brushes or spatulas with it, which is easier for children to handle.
	Wallpaper paste is cheap and good for sticking paper to paper. It can be used with a brush, making it easier for children to control.

Materials for cutting and sticking

Collages

A collage is a piece of art made by sticking different materials onto paper. It is fun, easy to do and creative. It can be a picture (e.g. of the beach) but it does not have to be. It is a way of expressing what you like and enjoy.

You can use fabric, paper, feathers, lace, wool and photos – anything you want. When doing a collage with a young child, be sure not to use buttons or small items that they may put into their mouths.

If you want to make a picture, it might be an idea to find out what the child would like to do, but have some ideas yourself.

Ideas include: a field with trees and sheep, a house and garden, a beach with boats, umbrellas and sandcastles, mountains and snow, a clown, a snowman.

- Use a fairly large piece of card for the background.
- Use coloured card for the background wherever possible – otherwise try painting it.
- Sketch out a simple design onto the background.
- Once the child starts cutting and sticking, give advice and help only when needed.

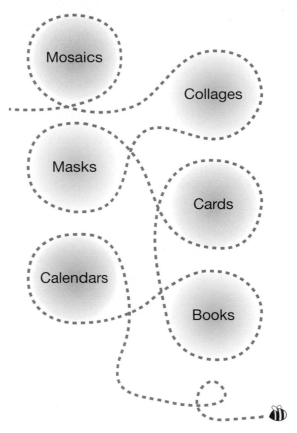

Ideas for cutting and sticking

Children enjoy making collages with coloured strips of paper

> **!** **Remember**
>
> Don't do it for them!

Making cards

Cards can be made for all sorts of occasions (e.g. birthday, Christmas, Mother's Day, get well soon). The same ideas can be used to make party invitations.

- Cut out and stick on pictures from old birthday or Christmas cards.
- Draw a picture of a simple shape (e.g. a flower, a boat, balloons). Scrunch up small pieces of tissue paper and stick inside the shapes.
- Cut simple shapes out of a piece of card and stick tissue paper or cellophane behind to give a stained-glass window effect.

You could use a computer to help the child to write a message for inside the card.

Children enjoy making cards for someone special

Making masks

Children love making and wearing masks – either of people or animals. They can be decorated with fabric, feathers, coloured tissue paper, foil, sequins, etc. Detail can be added with paints and crayons.

Wool or fabric can be used for hair. The masks can then be used in imaginative play.

- Make the basic shape out of card – roll it into a tube first so it will fit the shape of the head more easily.

- Make holes in each side, thread elastic through and fasten.
- Cut out eye holes and perhaps nose and mouth holes.
- Decorate.

You could also make masks from paper plates (not paper bags).

Fun face masks

Mosaics

Mosaics are made by cutting or tearing small pieces of coloured paper and sticking them onto paper to make a pattern or shape.

Tissue paper is good for this because it can be scrunched up into balls and then stuck down. This gives a 3D effect.

- Cut or tear up pieces of paper and sort into colours (this will encourage sorting skills and colour recognition).
- Draw a simple pattern or a simple shape onto card or paper – for example, a flower, a clown, a sheep or a boat.
- Decide on the colours to use.
- Stick the coloured paper onto the background to make the mosaic.

Making snowflakes

Once children can use scissors fairly accurately to snip, they will enjoy making snowflakes. Use different coloured tissue paper so that it is easy for them to cut.

- Cut out fairly large circles – use a plate as a guide.
- Fold the circle in half, then in half again, and then again.
- Snip small pieces out of each side.
- Open out to form the 'snowflake'.

These could then be stuck onto a larger piece of card and you could add a frame to make a picture.

Model making

Children of all ages enjoy making shapes (modelling) from materials such as play dough, salt dough and even boxes. Younger children will just enjoy feeling, squeezing and stretching them into different shapes. Older children can use different tools to help shape the dough, such as blunt knives or shape cutters.

Patterns can be stamped on the dough using forks, cotton reels, stampers, etc.

How model making can help learning and development

Physical development

Gross motor skills

Rolling, squashing, squeezing, pinching and shaping the dough will:

- strengthen arm muscles and fingers
- improve fine motor skills
- improve hand–eye coordination
- teach children how to use different tools and equipment correctly.

Sensory skills

Develops sensory skills of:

- touch
- sight
- smell.

Intellectual – concepts

Children will learn:

- different shapes and sizes when making shapes
- to use their imagination
- to develop creative skills
- the difference between materials
- the properties of materials.

Intellectual – language

- Learn new words to describe colour, texture, shapes, etc.
- Will enjoy talking about what they are doing.
- Ask questions.

Social development

- Children often like to do this sort of activity on their own.
- Learning to accept safety and hygiene rules.

Emotional development

- Rolling, squeezing, punching and shaping can all help to get rid of aggression (negative emotions).
- Will have fun and enjoy themselves.
- May feel good about what they have made – improve self-confidence and self-esteem.
- May feel more independent.
- Can be relaxing.

Other areas

- Numeracy.
- Using numbers to count.
- Understanding shapes.
- Making patterns.
- Size.
- Learning that different materials have different properties.

Planning

Quite young children will enjoy this sort of activity – those as young as eighteen months to two years can squeeze and stretch the dough, provided they have passed the 'mouthing' stage (putting everything into their mouths).

Don't expect too much of children. They may not be able to make a shape or object that you can recognise until they are about four or five!

Using salt dough encourages sensory development and fine motor skills

18 months–2½ years	Will enjoy handling and squeezing dough.
	May be able to copy making a sausage shape.
	May be able to decorate a piece of dough with different marks, if shown.
3–4 years	May begin to roll out, cut and make simple shapes.
	Handling and squeezing the dough is probably still more important than making shapes.
4–5 years	Will be able to make things, such as bowls and snakes.
	Will enjoy using different objects to make marks on the dough.

Stages of model making

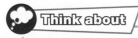

Making models can be a messy activity. Think about:
- where you will do the activity
- covering work surfaces
- wearing protective clothing
- safety.

You can buy play dough and other modelling materials, but it can be expensive. It is cheap and easy to make your own. You could even make it with the child.

Play dough

Below is a basic recipe that can be used for all sorts of modelling activities. If stored correctly, it will keep for several weeks.

Play dough

Ingredients

100 g plain flour
50 g salt
1 teaspoon cream of tartar
1 teaspoon oil
150 ml water
1–2 teaspoons food colouring

Method

1. Put flour, salt and cream of tartar into a bowl. Add oil and food colouring to the water.
2. Gradually add the water to the dry ingredients – beat well to remove any lumps.
3. Cook over a low heat, stirring all the time, until the dough forms a ball that leaves the sides of the pan clean.
4. Put onto a lightly floured, flat surface to cool (soak the pan!).
5. Knead until smooth and stretchy.

- Make up batches of differently coloured dough, e.g. blue, red, yellow and green.
- Add glitter to make the dough sparkle.
- Store by wrapping in cling film and keeping in an airtight container in the fridge.

Salt dough

Salt dough is similar to play dough, but it can be baked so that it goes hard (this can take a long time). It can be painted and varnished to make it last.

Salt dough

Ingredients

100 g plain flour
50 g salt
80 ml water
1 teaspoon oil or glycerine

Method

1. Put flour, salt and oil into a bowl. Add the water little by little to make a smooth, stretchy but not sticky dough.
2. Put onto a floured surface. Knead until smooth and use to make models.
3. Bake at 120°C/Gas mark ½ until firm (2–3 hours depending on thickness).
4. Paint the finished models. You could paint the model with PVA glue to give a shiny finish.

top tip

You can air-dry small items – just leave them on a flat surface – but it will take about 48 hours.

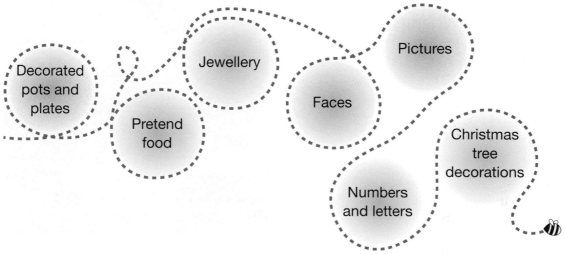

Ideas for modelling with play and salt dough

Junk modelling

Children of all ages are fascinated by cardboard boxes and wrapping paper, and will play happily with them for hours. Younger children will use boxes as containers, and fill and empty them with bricks or other toys.

By the time children are two-and-a-half to three years old, they will be developed enough to be ready to try junk modelling. Junk modelling is making models out of different household items, such as empty cereal boxes or yoghurt cartons.

At 2½ years	Children will only be able to make very simple models and will need help with ideas and making.
By 3½–4 years	They will be more skilled and imaginative, will want to choose for themselves and will be able to work more on their own, but they will still need advice and support at times.

Stages of junk modelling

Planning

Because junk modelling is similar to cutting and sticking and collage work, preparation and organisation for this activity is very much the same.

You need to collect a good range of junk materials (see below) and choose a suitable space for the activity.

Creating a junk model

What about materials?

To make	Empty cereal boxes and biscuit boxes of different sizes, shoe boxes, pizza boxes, kitchen roll holders, egg boxes, yoghurt cartons, margarine or butter containers, plastic bottles, bubble wrap, cotton reels, jar lids.
For sticking	PVA glue, brushes, sticky tape, string, paperclips, rubber bands; staples and split pins are best used only by adults.
To decorate	Paints, crayons, tissue, felt pens, buttons, cotton wool balls, sequins, wool, pieces of fabric, glitter, etc.

Materials for junk modelling

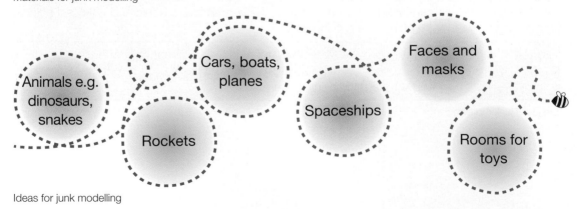

Ideas for junk modelling

Dressing up

Children enjoy dressing up from an early age. Young children who may not be able to dress themselves can take part in simple role play with the help of an adult, e.g. by wearing a policeman's helmet.

Children could use any of the following to develop their imagination and role play:

- old clothing
- accessories, e.g. hats, gloves, shoes
- shop-bought outfits, including well-known characters, e.g. Spiderman, Superman, Cinderella
- jewellery – this could be an adult's old, unwanted junk jewellery or the child could make their own
- props, e.g. a medical bag with a stethoscope
- the child's own baby clothing used on their doll or teddy
- face paints bought from specialist shops.

Children can play on their own or with a small group of children, and often without much help from adults. Children will develop their own characters and storylines in their role play.

Popular outfits

Many different well-known character outfits are worn and played with. This allows children to act out stories from books, videos and television programmes that they have watched.

A dressing-up box

Children like to open a box full of dressing-up clothes and choose an outfit. This allows a group of children to learn to share and agree over who should wear what. It also encourages their imaginations.

Face painting

Specialist face paints can be used to develop a character or role. Children love to paint each other's faces when they get older.

Dressing up for pretend play

> **! Remember**
>
> Safety:
> → Items that have sharp edges or small items that could be a choking hazard, such as loose buttons, are not suitable for children under the age of three.
> → If dressing-up items are too big or long, they could cause a child to trip.
> → Cords, ties and belts could be dangerous if used by an unsupervised child because they could accidentally strangle themselves.
> → Face paints should conform to British Safety Standards. Always check with parents first to see if their child is allergic to the paints.

Making dens

Dens can be made both inside and outside – if the weather is good and the area safe! Making the den is one type of imaginative play – using it as a place to act out roles or stories or plan adventures is another. Dressing up may be part of the activity as well.

To make a den inside, tablecloths, towels, old sheets, old curtains, etc. can be draped over chairs, clothes dryers/airers and furniture. Toys and other accessories may then be moved inside the den or items made for the den from boxes, tins, etc.

When planning a den, choose a corner of the room that is not in the way so that parents will allow the den to be kept for a while.

Making dens – great fun!

Outside dens can be made in the garden, again using old sheets, curtains, rugs or tablecloths draped over plastic garden furniture.

> **! Remember**
>
> Children must be supervised for these sorts of activities.

Children may also have shop-bought tents that make instant dens. For example:
- a fairy castle
- the jungle
- a car
- a train.

More expensive wooden chalets and bought Wendy houses also provide areas for children to develop their imaginations. However, children often prefer the den that they have made themselves.

Small world play

Small world play involves children playing with small characters and/or items. This type of play gives the child the opportunity to see a whole scene – for example, a farm with animals, tractors, a field and fencing. The child may begin by creating part of the scene, such as a cow in a field, and then develop a more complicated scene with a storyline.

Children will often construct towns, buildings, cars, etc. from building bricks and construction toys such as Lego® or Duplo®, then use toys and toy cars to act out stories.

Bought small world toys – for example, garages, hospitals, space stations, zoos and shops, and the people who live in them – will give children hours of fun and lots of

Small world play lets children make up their own stories

opportunities to make up stories and act out situations.

On a beach or in a garden, children will often build towns, castles, farms, houses and gardens by using sand or soil, and marking out roads and tracks. Flowers and twigs will become trees, and pebbles can be people or cars.

Toy shops sell a wide variety of small world play items.

Using boxes and other household objects

Cardboard and other types of boxes and containers can be used to develop imaginative play. This is a cheap way of using a material that is no longer needed. The cardboard is usually strong, already in a box shape, sometimes with a lid, and comes in various sizes.

Types of cardboard boxes include cereal boxes, old shoe boxes and large cardboard boxes from a supermarket.

Some ideas

With a little imagination, cardboard boxes can become many different things. Some ideas are given below.

Small boxes

- animals
- hotel
- furniture for doll's house
- secret garden
- miniature garden
- car for teddy
- train for doll
- shop till

Large boxes

- shop counter
- car
- boat
- train
- bed
- kennel
- doll's house
- table

> **! Remember**
>
> → Check for staples that might hurt children.
> → Adults may need to help children use scissors.

Children may want to develop these ideas further by painting the box to add more detail. The following materials could be used:

- safety scissors
- wool
- paint/paintbrushes
- foil paper/tissue paper
- glue/sticky tape
- beads.

Playing shops

To play shops, tins and small packets from the cupboard can be used, with a parent's permission. A tablecloth put over the top of a table is a simple way to display the goods. A till made from a shoe box with pretend money that the child has made, or a toy till with toy money, will make the shop more realistic. The shop may also sell cakes, biscuits or crafts that you have made.

Playing shops can help children to learn number concepts

Puppets

Puppets can be made from clean, old socks. Buttons, bands, felt tip pens and paint can be used for faces; wool for hair; and odd scraps of material for clothing. Socks and tights filled with old washed tights make great heads for puppets. Shop-bought glove puppets, string puppets and finger puppets can also develop children's imaginations. A home-made theatre could be made from a box.

Shadow puppets can be made cheaply with the use of a torch or bright light that can create patterns or images on the wall of a room and can be used to help make up stories at bedtime.

Simple sock puppets will give hours of fun

 Think about

Toilet roll tubes may not be hygienic so try using kitchen roll tubes instead.

Dolls and soft toys

Most children are bought lots of soft toys, animals, dolls and books, and often have large collections. These are great for pretend play and children will use them to act out roles from their own families. They might copy what they see mum and dad doing in real life – for example, cooking a meal, mending the car or gardening. Soft toys also provide great emotional support.

Children act out roles in pretend play

Dolls and soft toys can be used to act out the following situations:

- the garage
- parties
- the circus
- the café
- the zoo
- school or nursery
- the hospital
- the library
- picnics.

Picnics, and tea and birthday parties

Children love to play at tea parties and birthday parties, sometimes with real food or just by pretending. They like to put real drinks into a cup and pretend that cold water is a hot drink.

Tea parties could take place on a small child's table with a miniature

tea set. Teddies and dolls may be asked for tea or join in games and pretend to be at a party. A pretend birthday cake and candles can make the whole event more exciting.

The tea party or picnic could take place on a rug or towel placed in an imaginary field or the child's garden if the weather is fine.

Outdoor play

Children need to be allowed and encouraged to play outdoors as much as possible. Not only is it a great way to develop physical skills, especially gross motor skills, it can also help prevent obesity and health problems, such as type 2 diabetes. Running around also burns off excess energy and makes you feel good!

Planning

When planning and organising outdoor activities, it is very important to think carefully about safety, as well as how you think it will help the child to learn and develop.

 Remember

> With outdoor play, the child must be supervised at all times, so careful planning is needed.

- Where will you go and how you will get there?
- What facilities are available?
- Check to see if it is suitable for the age of your child – visit first.
- Carry out a risk assessment.
- Make sure the child is wearing suitable clothing.

Most importantly:

- Get permission from the parents.

Ideas for outdoor play

Playing in the garden can offer lots of opportunities for different kinds of outdoor play. Often children will have swings, slides or climbing frames but, if not, there are lots of different activities you could plan.

Not all families have a garden or outside space to play safely. Parks and play areas give children the chance to experience outdoor play and to meet other children.

Riding a bike

- Helps to strengthen leg muscles and bones.
- Improves balance.
- Builds up stamina.
- Helps coordination.
- Increases confidence.

Playing hide-and-seek or chase

- Develops coordination and balance.
- Builds up stamina.
- Improves spatial awareness.
- Develops social skills.
- Strengthens muscles and bones.

Hopping, skipping and jumping

- Develops leg muscles.
- Improves coordination and balance.
- Improves stamina.
- Builds up confidence.

Playing with a football, bat and ball or skittles

- Develops hand–eye coordination.
- Develops arm and leg muscles.
- Encourages cooperative play.
- Improves stamina.

Climbing

- Improves balance and coordination.
- Develops problem solving.
- Develops arm and leg muscles.
- Increases confidence.

Playing with snowballs or building a snowman

- Increases strength in arm and leg muscles.
- Improves coordination.
- Encourages imaginative play.

All of these activities will give children the chance to 'let off steam'. Fresh air will also help them to sleep better and improve their appetite.

Other ideas for outdoor play:

- Make stepping stones out of pieces of card and place them around the garden – get the child to walk across the stones.
- Go for a walk in the country or on the beach. Collect interesting objects, e.g. leaves, shells. Use these to make a collage when you get home.
- Play hopscotch.
- Create a small garden for the child to look after. Plant some quick-growing seeds.
- Take a trip to the beach to build sandcastles.
- Play in a paddling pool.
- Mix soil and water to make mud.
- Plan a treasure hunt in the garden.

Ideas for younger children:
- A trip to the park.
- Play in a paddling pool filled with plastic coloured balls.
- Sit on a blanket and play with a soft ball.

Sand and water

Playing with sand and water develops many skills. It involves messy play, creative play and uses natural materials. It also encourages children to begin to develop problem-solving skills as they experiment with designs and learn through trial and error – for example, building dams and castles.

How sand and water play can help learning and development

Physical development
- Hand–eye coordination, pouring water into vessels.
- Control and strengthening of muscles in the hands and arms.
- Fine motor skills with spreading, spooning, etc.
- Drawing in the sand.

Sensory
- Development of touch/texture.

Intellectual – concepts
- Organisational skills, sequence and patterns.
- Learning about natural materials.
- Pouring water/sand into different-sized vessels develops the concepts of size, shape, capacity, volume.
- Understanding floating and sinking.
- Creative development, using materials imaginatively.
- Understanding rules about safety and danger.
- Problem solving.

Social development
- Sharing space, equipment.
- Understanding personal hygiene rules.
- Thinking about others.
- Learning to play cooperatively.

Intellectual – language
- Improves the vocabulary with new words, e.g. splish, splash.
- Develops descriptive language.
- Language used to negotiate.

Emotional development
- Develops a sense of fun and enjoyment.
- Children gain confidence.

Planning

Choose activities carefully.

- Activities must be suitable for the age of the child.
- Activities must be approved by the parent/carer. Will the activity be too messy? This type of activity can only take place with parental support.
- Activities must be neither too easy nor too difficult.

Once you have chosen what to do, you need to check:

- equipment needed
- hygiene of the equipment
- when the activity will take place
- safety
- allergies the child may have to touching any materials.

Playing with sand

Playing with sand does not require a sand pit – an old washing-up bowl, tyre, seed tray or any other suitable container could be used. Clean and cheap play sand can be bought from toy shops. Or if you live near to a beach, plan a visit there, but get the parents to go with you.

Sand play can also be used in imaginative play using small world figures, such as people, animals, dinosaurs and cars.

Remember

Wet and dry sand are different so try to let children play with both.

A range of objects can be used when playing with sand, such as:

- buckets and spades
- moulds
- yoghurt pots
- set of old scales
- shapes
- trucks and diggers.

Remember

Outdoor sand pits should be covered. This is to prevent animals contaminating the sand and to stop water collecting inside, which could be dangerous if a toddler fell in.

Sand encourages physical, imaginative and discovery play

Playing with water

Water activities could take place in the bath, in a clean washing-up bowl, with a bucket, in a paddling pool or in the kitchen sink. It could get very messy so check with an adult before you start.

What you might need:

- plastic bottles
- jugs and containers
- colander
- sieve
- toy tea set
- sponge
- whisk
- funnel.

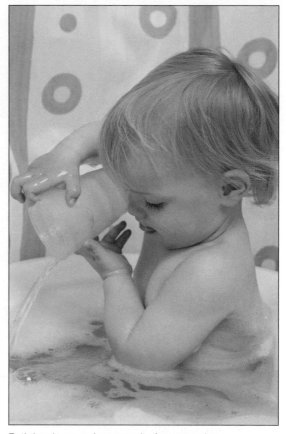

Bathtime is a good opportunity for water play

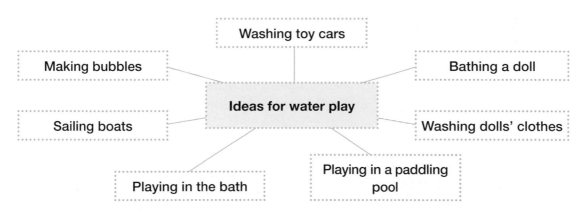

Washing toy cars

Making bubbles

Bathing a doll

Ideas for water play

Sailing boats

Washing dolls' clothes

Playing in the bath

Playing in a paddling pool

Using lots of plastic equipment, e.g. cups, bowls, watering cans and sieves, children can play for hours enjoying the fresh air and developing their skills. In the warmer weather, children love to play outside in the garden using a paddling pool, hose pipe and sprinkler or even an old baby bath.

Magic! It goes in there and comes out there!

Playing with bubbles is also great fun. A variety of simple containers could be used. Straws are good to make bubbles with and there is a variety of play products in toy shops to assist with this type of play.

Food and cooking

Preparing, cooking and, of course, eating food is an activity that children can enjoy from an early age – and one that can help many areas of development and learning.

Through handling food, they can begin to understand about different countries and cultures, healthy eating, science and maths, weighing and measuring, hygiene and safety, and how to be creative and imaginative. The list is endless and, of course, they get to eat the end product.

How cooking activities can help learning and development

Physical development

Gross motor skills are developed by:
- kneading bread mixtures
- rolling out biscuits and pastry
- beating and stirring cake mixtures
- lifting ingredients to weigh out
- pouring ingredients into bowl
- cutting out shapes.

Fine motor skills are developed by:
- measuring ingredients
- weighing ingredients
- spooning mixture into cases
- cracking eggs into bowls
- decorating cakes
- cutting up fruit and vegetables
- spreading fillings on bread or biscuits
- icing cakes and biscuits
- decorating pizzas
- cutting out shapes for biscuits.

Develops sensory skills of:
- touch
- smell
- sight.

Social development

Learning to work with others.
- Sharing, taking turns and cooperating.
- Importance of hygiene and safety.
- Likes and dislikes.

Emotional development

Gives opportunities to experience both positive and negative emotions.
- Helps to learn to control negative emotions, e.g. anger, frustration.
- Patience.

Intellectual – concepts

Cooking activities can help develop concepts of:
- size
- shape
- number
- weight
- bigger/smaller
- colour.

Intellectual – language

New words for equipment and ingredients.
- Describing and comparing words.
- Asking questions and following instructions.
- Talking to others.
- Specialist words, e.g. creaming.

Other areas

Numeracy
- Volume, weight and measurement when weighing and measuring.
- Sizes, e.g. bowls, spoons, cutters.
- Shapes when cutting out.
- Counting.
- Comparing sizes and shapes.
- Timing.
- Estimating, e.g. when dividing mixtures into cases.

Science
- Understanding solids and liquids.
- How foods change when cooked or frozen.
- Effect of heat.

Health and safety
- Understanding safety rules.
- Understanding hygiene rules.

Planning

Don't think that food activities, and especially 'cooking', can only be done with older children. You don't always have to use an oven, microwave or sharp knives. With a little thought, imagination and careful planning, young children will get just as much fun and enjoyment out of making something that involves no cooking at all, as long as they are 'doing'. No child wants to sit and watch you do all the exciting bits!

Cooking
- Cakes
- Biscuits
- Scones
- Bread
- Toast
- Pizza
- Soups
- Popcorn

Cooling and freezing
- Refrigerator biscuits
- Milk shakes
- Jellies
- Trifles

Food activities do not have to involve cooking

Spreading and decorating
- Sandwiches
- Cakes
- Pizza
- Biscuits

Shaping
- Pasta
- Biscuits
- Sweets

Cutting and preparing
- Fruit salad
- Salads
- Soups

Any food or cooking activity needs to be planned very carefully. Like any other activity, you need to choose something that the child will enjoy and can succeed in, and that will help their learning and development.

You must also think about health and safety.

Planning points	Yes	No
Is my choice too easy?		
Is my choice too difficult?		
Will my child enjoy it?		
Will it take too long?		
Is there plenty for my child to do?		
Have I thought about safety?		
Have I checked with the parents?		

You might need:

- permission from parents
- suitable recipe
- ingredients
- baking tray
- oven gloves
- rolling pin
- non-breakable bowls
- tablespoon, teaspoon and wooden spoon
- palette knife
- apron
- scales
- cooling tray.

Choosing recipes

You can buy packet mixes to make cakes, but making your own is better. They taste good, they have no additives and the child can learn so much more by weighing and measuring for themselves.

Recipes should be quite simple and easy to make. There should only be a few ingredients and not too many different stages. Recipe books written for children are a good place to look. Think about how long things will take to cook. Children are not always patient, so think about what you might do while the food is cooking. It might not always be safe or practical to do the washing up!

Small cakes

These are quick and easy to make and cook. You could also add some cocoa, cherries or dried fruit to them.

Ingredients

100 g self-raising flour
100 g castor sugar
100 g soft butter or margarine
2 eggs

Method

1. Put 12 cake cases into a tray.
2. Put all the ingredients into a mixing bowl. Beat everything together with a wooden spoon until creamy.
3. Divide the mixture evenly between the cake cases.
4. Bake for 15–20 minutes.

Makes – 12
Oven – Gas 4 or 180°C
Cooking time – 15–20 minutes

Shortbread biscuits

This is an easy recipe with only three main ingredients. You can use biscuit or scone cutters to cut out the shapes or use special biscuit cutters in different shapes, e.g. animals, Christmas shapes.

Ingredients

150 g plain flour
50 g castor sugar
100 g butter or margarine

Method

1. Put the sugar and butter or margarine into a bowl. Beat together with a wooden spoon until soft and creamy.
2. Sift the flour into the mixture and stir to make a soft dough.
3. Knead into a ball and roll out.
4. Cut out shapes and place on a greased baking tray (use a palette knife to lift).
5. Bake for 15–20 minutes, until a light golden brown.

Oven – Gas 4 or 180°C
Cooking time – 15–20 minutes

Decorating cakes and biscuits

Butter icing is often easier for children to make and easier to spread on cakes and biscuits than glacé icing – both can be coloured.

With older children, you could use ready-made
fondant icing. This can be coloured and rolled into different shapes.

Use chocolate buttons, sweets, sugar strands, chocolate vermicelli, cherries, liquorice laces, etc. for decorations.

Practice makes perfect!

Butter icing

Ingredients

100 g butter or margarine
200 g icing sugar
1 tsp milk

Method

1. Put the butter or margarine into a bowl and beat until soft.
2. Sift the icing sugar into the softened butter and mix well.
3. Add a little milk to make it creamy.

Bread and pizza

Making and shaping bread is great fun and gives children practice at developing a number of physical skills, especially fine motor skills

It does, however, take a long time to make bread so it might be a good idea to buy a packet mix for this.

Younger children will enjoy being able to handle and shape dough into interesting shapes, such as hedgehogs, snails, tortoises, flowers and letters.

Older children will enjoy making their own pizza.

Glacé icing

Ingredients

100 g icing sugar
Approximately 1 tbsp warm water

Method

1. Sift the icing sugar into a small bowl.
2. Add warm water a little at a time and keep stirring until a thick smooth paste is formed.

Pizza

Ingredients

1 packet bread mix
Tomato purée

Selection of toppings e.g. cheese, sliced ham, pieces of sliced pepper, mushrooms, sweetcorn, sliced pepperoni, etc.

Method

1. Make the bread up following the instructions on the packet.
2. Divide into four pieces. Roll each piece out to a circle approximately 15 cm across.
3. Spread each circle with 1 tablespoon of tomato purée.
4. Decorate the pizzas. Bake for 10–15 minutes.

Makes – four small pizzas
Oven – Gas 7 or 220°C
Cooking time – 10–15 minutes

Other ideas for food activities

Cress eggheads

You will need:

- eggs
- an eggcup
- felt tip pens
- tissue or paper towels or cotton wool
- cress seeds.

Eggciting!

What to do

1. Put an egg into boiling water for three minutes until softly boiled and put into an eggcup. Carefully cut the top off the egg. Your child can eat the egg for a snack.

2. Gently scrape out any remaining bits of egg and clean the shell as carefully as possible, then fill with cotton wool. If using tissue or paper towels, tear into small pieces.

3. Leave a gap of 1 cm from the top.

4. Moisten the paper or cotton wool and sprinkle on a thin layer of cress seeds.

5. Put the egg in the light and leave for two or three days for the seeds to sprout. Make sure you sprinkle it with water each day.

6. When the cress is fully grown, you could use it to make egg and cress sandwiches with the child.

Play dough

Make play dough into food shapes, bake and paint. Use in imaginative play, e.g. parties, cafés and restaurants, shops.

Shopping

Take the child on a shopping trip to the supermarket and let them help to choose simple items. Collect food packaging and set up a shop/supermarket – pretend play.

Eating plates

Collect coloured pictures of different foods from magazines. Stick onto paper plates to make healthy/unhealthy meals. This will help fine motor skills and knowledge of healthy eating.

Make a food book

Use cut-out pictures from magazines or clip-art from a computer to make a book about foods for a child.

Eating out

Take the child to a café or restaurant. This will help social and emotional development, as well as fine motor skills.

Books and stories

Books are probably one of the most important 'toys' a child will ever have. Children are never too young to 'read' a book; there are lots of different types and kinds of books to suit all ages and they can be read anytime, anywhere, and they can be enjoyed over and over again.

Long before children can actually 'read', they are learning how books are used – that pages are turned over from right to left, that words usually go across a page from left to right and that pages are usually read from top to bottom.

There are two ways books could be used in your child study visits:

1. You or the child could choose a book or books to read.
2. You could make a book. This could be either *for* the child or *with* the child.

Reading a book

Although most children enjoy reading books, you need to plan this activity just as carefully as any other. If it is a sunny day, they might not want to sit indoors quietly reading!

How books and stories can help learning and development

Physical development

- Turning pages, following the words with fingers and pointing to pictures all help fine motor skills and hand–eye coordination.
- Looking at books and handling them helps sensory development (touch and sight).
- Sense of touch is developed when using books with different textures.
- Sitting still requires physical control.

Intellectual – concepts

- Encourages imagination and creativity.
- Helps to develop memory skills.
- Helps children learn to concentrate.
- Will help to develop an understanding of different concepts, e.g. numbers, letters, colours, size, shape, time.
- Increases knowledge and understanding of their own world and wider world.

Social development

- Helps children to bond with parents.
- Children get to spend quality individual time with people.
- Books can help children begin to know what is right and wrong.
- Reading can encourage sharing and taking turns.

Emotional development

- Provides enjoyment and pleasure.
- Being able to read gives children confidence.
- Being able to read makes children more independent.
- Reading with parents makes children feel loved and secure.
- Children can begin to understand their own feelings through characters in stories.

Other areas

- Books can help children to learn about and understand a huge range of subjects.
- Develop an awareness of being able to use books as reference and research material.

Intellectual – language

- Learn new words.
- Encourage children to ask questions.
- Improve listening skills.

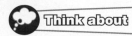

You should think about:
- the age and stage of development of the child
- the length of the book – young children cannot concentrate for a long time
- the language used – this should be suitable for the age of the child
- the sort of pictures used – these can help the child to follow and understand the story
- what it is about – think about what the child might enjoy; younger children need simple stories
- stories with rhymes and actions – children can then join in
- using different voices and facial expressions when reading
- using toys to 'act out' stories
- choosing a comfortable, quiet area to read with them, away from the TV
- going to the library and letting the child choose new books
- drawing pictures about the story or characters.

Making a book for or with a child

Before planning and making a book, either for or with a child, think about why you are doing it and what you hope the child will learn from it. This will help you to write your aims and expectations.

For example, you might want to use the book to test what the child knows or to help them learn something new or be able to understand something better, e.g. numbers, letters, shapes, colours, counting; or you might want it to be more of a creative activity, involving cutting and sticking, painting, drawing and colouring in.

You should think about:
- the age, stage of development and skills of the child
- what they are interested in
- using simple shapes
- using bright colours
- where you will make it
- what materials you will need
- how long it will take
- any safety measures you will need to take.

You could buy a cheap scrapbook or make your own book from paper or thin card, punched and held together with string or wool. A5 or A4 size is probably best. Sugar paper is also useful because it can be bought in different colours, and is cheap and quite thick so easier to handle.

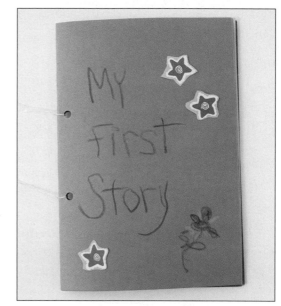

Depending on what sort of book you are making, you will need glue (see cutting and sticking, page 67), pencils, crayons, felt tips, pictures, photographs, small pieces of fabric, tissue paper, etc.

You could also put each page into a plastic wallet to make it stronger and easy to wipe clean.

Ideas for making books:

* Make a book using pictures from old birthday or Christmas cards.
* Make a 'how many' book to help the child recognise shapes and learn to count.
* Make a zigzag book, which can be hung down or will stand up. Fold a long strip of paper like a concertina. Either put different drawings on each page (e.g. animals, letters, numbers, everyday objects) or put one simple object, like a flower, which 'grows' when opened out.
* Make up a simple story using your child as the main character – the child could make up the story and you could write it down.
* Make a colouring book.
* Make a scrapbook about your child. Put in pictures of the child, family, any pets, favourite toys, colours, nursery rhymes, songs, and so on.
* Make a join-the-dots book.
* Make an alphabet scrapbook with pictures of objects beginning with each letter of the alphabet.
* Make an activity book.

Letters, words and numbers

Activities and games using letters and numbers are important because they are the first steps in starting to read and write. In the same way, activities and games can help children to begin to understand the concept of numbers and counting, both of which are important in developing maths skills as they get older.

Learning to recognise letters, words and numbers takes a long time and is mainly done through repetition. Making up games and activities using letters, numbers and words can make this more exciting.

Learning letters and words

Reading stories and looking at books are both important in helping children to begin to recognise letters and simple words. Action rhymes and songs can also help, as can putting labels onto objects around the home.

Making letter and picture cards

Cut some A4 card into rectangles – about 10 cm x 6 cm. You will need 16 (you could use old birthday cards).

Choose four simple words, e.g. ball, cup, sun and dog. Write each of these onto two cards. Now draw and colour in pictures to match the words on the other cards. Again you will need two of each one.

You can now use these cards in different ways:
- Playing snap.
- Matching the picture to the word. Match the pictures. Match the word to the picture.
- Turn the cards face down. Take turns in turning over two cards to make into pairs.

Picture lotto

Divide two pieces of A4 paper or card into six rectangles. Draw pictures of simple objects onto one sheet and the first letter of the object onto the other sheet.

Cut out the picture cards.
Get the child to try to match the pictures to the letter.

Word and picture dominoes

Cut some domino shapes approximately 15 cm x 6 cm. Put letters or simple words and pictures onto the cards.

  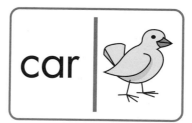

Spread them out on the floor or on a table, and get the child to try to match them up.

Alphabet book

Write each letter of the alphabet at the top of a sheet of paper. Draw or stick pictures of objects beginning with that letter onto the page.

Letter frieze

Draw big outlines of letters onto pieces of card or paper. Let the child colour them in. Join the letters together with string or wool to make the child's name.

Ideas for learning numbers

Number cards

Cut 12 card shapes approx 10 cm × 6 cm. On six of the cards, write the numbers 1–6 and colour them in. On the other

six, draw large spots, stars or simple objects to match each of the number cards and colour them in. Get the child to try to put each of the cards in sequence.

The child could also match the number cards to the spotted cards or you could take out one of the cards and ask the child which one is missing.

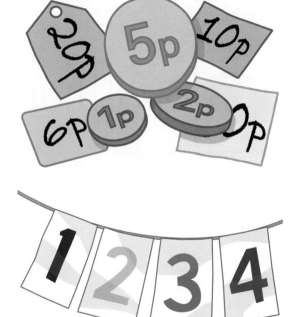

Shops

Make some cardboard coins of 1p, 2p, 5p, 10p.

Make some price labels for the child's toys or books with different prices.

Number wall frieze

Make a decorated wall frieze or bunting with your child. Write the numbers 1–10 onto separate sheets of paper or card. You could draw simple pictures to match the numbers and colour them in.

Games

There are lots of games that can be played with or by children, ranging from active games, such as football and hide-and-seek, to pretend/imaginative games where children make up the rules themselves, to board and card games, such as Snap or Lotto.

All are important in helping different areas of development. Many board and card games are competitive – sometimes these can cause arguments and tantrums and can lessen children's confidence and self-esteem if they lose. Most of these games have rules that have to be followed. They are important because they help children to learn how to:

- share
- take turns
- play fairly
- follow rules.

They also begin to teach children that they may not always win.

 **Remember**

> When planning to play board games and card games, remember that:
> → children under three years old will not be able to sit still or concentrate for a long time
> → children under three years old will not understand the idea of rules.

How some games can help learning and development

Physical development
- 'Simon says' can help develop gross motor skills and balance and coordination.
- Games such as snakes and ladders, Connect 4 or Lotto help fine motor skills and hand–eye coordination.

Intellectual – concepts
- Card games and matching games help memory skills and quick thinking.
- Matching games encourage children to recognise how things are similar and different.
- Many games help logical thinking.
- Dice games can help counting and number skills.
- Most games improve concentration.

Emotional development
- Learn to accept losing.
- May increase (or decrease) self-esteem and confidence.
- Will experience a variety of both positive and negative emotions.

Social development
- Learning to share.
- Learning to take turns.
- Cooperating with others.

Other areas

Numeracy
- Board and card games can develop maths concepts and use of mathematical language.

Intellectual – language
- Encourages communication with others.
- Can increase vocabulary.

Music

Children of all ages can enjoy music. Even before birth, a baby can hear sounds, and many pregnant women play music to help soothe the baby. From being born, young babies will often fall asleep when parents sing to them and rock them gently, and they will watch and listen to musical mobiles hanging over their cots.

Music is an important part of learning – singing simple songs helps children's speech and language development, and learning about rhythm can help with maths. Dancing and clapping to music helps physical development, and music also helps children to express themselves and improves their self-confidence.

Birth to twelve months	<ul><li>From three months, babies will respond to music by turning towards the sound.</li><li>By six months, they start to imitate sounds.</li><li>By nine months, they can react to familiar songs.</li><li>By twelve months, they begin to create sounds by banging toys and other objects.</li></ul>
Eighteen months to three years	<ul><li>From eighteen months, they may be able to move and respond to music.</li><li>They will know the difference between fast and slow, loud and quiet.</li><li>They will start to know and sing along to simple songs.</li><li>They may be able to play simple musical instruments, such as drums, shakers and toy keyboards.</li></ul>
Three to five years	<ul><li>They will be more interested in making music.</li><li>They understand more about pitch and rhythm.</li><li>Singing becomes more tuneful.</li><li>They can sing more complicated songs.</li><li>They enjoy making new sounds.</li><li>They enjoy dancing to music and become more coordinated.</li></ul>

Children love to hear music, and from a very early age they respond to musical toys, often with sound and movement. As the child develops, they are able to concentrate for longer and so listen to music for longer. From this, they can develop their creative and physical skills.

How music can help learning and development

Physical development

Action songs and dance develop:
- gross motor skills
- balance
- coordination
- spatial awareness.

Using keyboards and instruments develops:
- fine motor skills
- hand–eye coordination.

Music and movement develop the senses, especially:
- listening
- touch.

Music and movement improve:
- breathing
- muscle tone.

Singing and speaking rhythmically exercises the vocal chords.

Intellectual – concepts

Music and movement help to develop:
- creativity through moving to different sounds and rhythms
- imagination
- memory and concentration skills
- listening skills.

Making music can encourage children to:
- explore and experiment
- express ideas through sound
- develop numeracy skills.

Intellectual – language

- Improves and increases vocabulary.
- Develops knowledge of comparative language.
- Develops non-verbal communication.
- Develops voice tone, range and delivery.
- Encourages communication through facial expression and body movement.

Social development

When working together with other children, music and dance can encourage:
- taking turns and cooperating
- sharing
- consideration for others.

Music and movement from other countries and cultures can help develop understanding and respect for others.

Emotional development

Music and movement encourage children to:
- express and share emotions, thoughts and feelings
- relax
- increase confidence and self-esteem.

Other areas

- Equal opportunities – knowing about music and instruments from other cultures.
- Vibrating instruments can assist with the development of children with hearing difficulties.
- Music can help to calm children with special needs who respond well to it.

Singing

Most children love to sing along to songs and rhymes and will do this over and over again. Children do not need to be able to read to learn a song. By singing their favourite songs, they learn more about sound and how to use their voices, as well as develop their language skills.

Toddlers singing and clapping

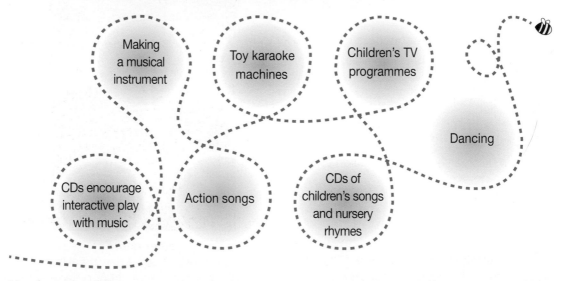

Making a musical instrument

Toy karaoke machines

Children's TV programmes

Dancing

CDs encourage interactive play with music

Action songs

CDs of children's songs and nursery rhymes

Ideas for music activities

Singing and clapping

Any game or song that requires clapping to a rhythm involves listening, repeating and recall. A child can copy an adult's actions. So stand up and let the child face you. For the child, this will be like looking into a mirror.

- Firstly, you do the actions to music and let the child copy.
- Secondly, you could ask the child to do their own actions and you can copy them.

Action songs

Here is an example of an action song that children might enjoy joining in with.

The Wheels on the Bus	Action
The wheels on the bus go round and round, round and round, round and round The wheels on the bus go round and round All day long	Children move their hands in a circle to show the wheel going round
Other verses can be made up to suit the situation. For example:	
The daddies (or mummies) on the bus go chatter, chatter, chatter	Fingers open and shut
The people on the bus go up and down	Jump up and down
The bell on the bus goes dingalingaling	Pretend to ring a bell
The windscreen wipers go swish, swish, swish	Move arms like wipers

Counting songs

Counting songs teach a child in a fun way to sequence numbers 1, 2, 3, 4, 5, and so on. They can also teach a child to count backwards. Children can use their fingers to do this, either on their own or by copying you.

AQA HOME ECONOMICS FOR GCSE: CHILD DEVELOPMENT – CONTROLLED ASSESSMENT GUIDE

Five little ducks

Five little ducks went swimming one day
Over the hills and far away
Mother duck said 'quack, quack, quack'
And four little ducks came swimming right back

Then continue…

Four little ducks, etc. …
Three little ducks, etc. …
Two little ducks, etc. …
One little duck, etc.

Making musical instruments

Musical instruments can be made from lots of household objects. Children under the age of five like to play with percussion instruments and they cost very little to make.

Drums

The following household containers make good drums:

- tins – empty and clean
- cake tins
- saucepans
- plastic bowls
- margarine tubs.

For the drumsticks, wooden spoons, metal spoons and pastry brushes all make great sounds. Drumstick heads can be made by adding sponge, paper, etc.

Household objects can become musical instruments

Shakers

To make shakers, you will need a container, such as a plastic bottle with a screw top or a tin with lid (e.g. cocoa tin, small box).

The best materials to fill the containers are dried pulses (e.g. peas, beans), rice, dried pasta, buttons, milk bottle tops and beads. Put a lid onto the container and seal with tape.

 Remember

> Making homemade instruments often means using uncooked pulses (e.g. peas), so children must be supervised to prevent accidents.

Dancing

All children love to dance, on their own or together. Using a CD player, you could play a selection of different types of music (e.g. fast and slow, high pitch and low pitch, loud and soft). Children often like to stand on your feet and dance around with you.

Some children go to formal classes (e.g. ballet, tap, modern dancing). They may like to put on their special shoes and clothes to show you how to do the dances.

Exercises to music

Children love to be active and especially like doing simple exercises to music, e.g. stretching and bending, arms stretched high in the air, bending forwards or sideways. Children could do star-jumps or bend their knees to the music. This develops a good sense of balance and rhythm.

Have a disco party

Get a torch, draw the curtains, turn off the lights and turn on the torch. Put on some lively music and have your own disco party.

Computers and hand-held games

Computers and hand-held games are enjoyed by many children. Like television and DVDs, they can be entertaining, they can be educational, and they can help children to know and experience the wider world.

Computer learning is interactive and therefore great for young children.

CD-ROMs, Nintendo games and websites such as CBeebies (www.bbc.co.uk/cbeebies) can help develop language and number skills, and your child may have access to these.

These could be just one of a range of different play activities you might choose when observing your child but remember that too long spent in front of a computer screen can limit social, physical (gross motor skills) and language development – and children can become addicted.

Using a keyboard will help develop fine motor skills and recognition of numbers and letters. Computers with touch screens or concept keypads are also of great value to children with disabilities.

Activities for young babies

Studying a very young baby can be difficult. In their first three months, babies tend to sleep most of the time – sometimes 20 out of every 24 hours. They wake up only when they are hungry, cold or uncomfortable.

During this stage, they have very little control over their physical actions, although they can hold things. This is a reflex action. They can only focus on objects, such as toys, if they are held close to them (within 25 cm) and babies communicate mainly by crying.

From three months, development begins to speed up and is easier to recognise, and during the rest of their first year their main development will be physical.

This does not mean that you should ignore intellectual, emotional or social development because it will certainly be happening! However, from the moment they are born, babies learn through their senses – mainly by touching, tasting (mouthing), listening and seeing. So it is very important that they:

- have a lot of close physical contact (are held and cuddled)
- are spoken to when being fed, changed, bathed, held
- have lots of stimuli to look at when they are not being handled, e.g. mobiles, friezes and pictures on walls
- have lots of 'play' times with parents and carers.

Babies will also quickly learn to communicate in different ways – different tones of cries will mean different things, and they will begin to gurgle, babble, use jargon, etc. until they begin to speak their first words.

They learn to socialise – mainly with parents and close family – but then gradually begin to accept others.

Although emotional development may seem slow, they will begin to show a range of different feelings – from happiness and contentment to shyness, frustration and anxiety.

Although it might seem easier to plan activities for toddlers and children, it is important to remember that, unless babies are given lots of time and attention from parents and carers, and chances to play, they may not develop at an 'average' rate.

Planning activities

You need to think, choose and plan carefully. It is really important that you:

- know exactly what babies can be expected to do at different stages in the first three months (check in textbooks)
- think about how you could use their toys to help them develop skills
- understand that you may not always see a lot of change and progression. Because of this, you may have to plan to do similar activities over several visits so that you can observe how they have changed or improved.

> **By having things to touch, feel and hold**
>
> **How babies learn through their senses**
>
> **By having things to look at**   **By having things to listen to**

	Gross motor skills	Fine motor skills	Sensory
At birth	• Reflex actions, e.g. skipping or walking reflex	• Reflex actions, e.g. grasp reflex	• Reflex actions, e.g. startle reflex
At one month	• May begin to lift head when laid on tummy • Will enjoy kicking	• Opens hands	• Can see objects close to them (25 cm) • Moves head towards sound
At three months	• Learning to support head • Kicks vigorously • Moves head to look at what parents are doing	• Clasps hands together • Looks at hands and plays with fingers • Can hold a toy for a short time	• Can focus on toys • May turn in right direction • If name called, begins to look around
At six months	• Can sit if supported by cushions • Can roll over • May try to crawl	• Will pass toys from hand to hand • Grabs toys using whole-hand palmar grasp	• Puts all objects to mouth • Becoming alert and curious about what goes on around him

Think about

When planning activities and visits, try to look at what the baby can do now *and* what they should be able to do next. This should help you to choose activities that will encourage the next stage of development.

It can be a good idea to observe babies when they are being fed, are in the bath or are being changed and played with by their parents. This can help you to see exactly how they behave and react, and you can then compare this to 'average' milestones. You can also see how parents play with and encourage their baby's development. Do not be tempted to make these into three separate visits as you may not have enough to observe.

Ideas for activities with babies

The following are simple ideas for activities with a very young baby, which could help you look at some of the different areas of development.

Remember

→ Try to do three or four different activities or look at the baby's routine at each visit so you can check different areas of development.
→ Look at the baby's reactions carefully and write them down.

Encouraging vision and head movement

Hold a simple, brightly coloured toy or rattle close to the baby's face (25 cm). Slowly move the toy or rattle from side to side. As the baby gets better at this, move the toy further from side to side or try moving it up and down, backwards and forwards.

Encouraging vision, hearing and communication skills

Talk to your baby. Hold the baby carefully, supporting the neck but looking at your face. Talk to and smile at the baby – give the baby time to reply. Although they cannot speak, they will concentrate on your movements and begin to gurgle and smile.

New babies need to be held and talked to

Encouraging sight and fine motor skills

Try making a simple mobile to hang above a cot, or a toy that will stretch across the cot for the baby to look at and reach out to.

You could use a covered coat hanger for the mobile (e.g. tinsel) and strong elastic fastened to each side of the cot. Try to choose things that will show different sounds, textures and shapes. Some ideas are: ribbons, card cut into shapes or faces and decorated, Christmas tree baubles, shapes with different patterns, yoghurt pots, foil crumpled into shapes, spirals cut out of card. This will encourage the child to explore the senses.

Encouraging gross motor skills

Once babies begin to get stronger, encourage gross motor skills by putting favourite toys just out of reach – this will encourage them to roll over.

Encouraging sensory development

Once your baby can sit reasonably well, even if supported by cushions, make a feely bag or basket of items with different textures (not toys), e.g. face cloth, small plastic bottle filled with rice, large pine cone, large, clean, smooth stone, woollen pom-pom, clothes peg, hair brush.

✓ top tip

- Compare what you see to what textbooks say about development.
- Try the same activities at a later visit – perhaps after two months – to see how the baby has improved.

Other ideas for activities

- Sing simple songs and action rhymes to baby, e.g. pat-a-cake, round and round the garden, this little piggy.
- Once baby can hold a toy, give them something to bang on, e.g. wooden spoon on pans, cake tins.
- Try passing toys between you and the baby as you talk to them. This will encourage fine motor skills and taking turns.
- And of course do not forget to use baby's own toys. Look at what is played with, how and for how long.

Baby gyms help sensory development

Development of the child

In this section, you will find information on all four areas of development (physical, intellectual, emotional and social), plus ideas for toys and play activities. The section is organised according to age. This information will be useful when planning visits and activities.

Developmental milestones

The age and stage at which children grow and develop depends on many factors. When studying children's development, we usually refer to developmental milestones.

Developmental milestones are sets of skills that most children will be expected to do at a certain age. In this section, we are going to look at the major physical, intellectual, emotional and social milestones.

 Remember

> These milestones are only a guide – all children are different and individual and will develop at different rates.

Newborn babies

At birth, all babies are totally dependent on their parents, but from the moment they are born they begin to learn and explore the world around them. They do this through their senses.

Although they can only focus on objects held close to them (25 cm), when awake they will look around, watch and, when held, focus intently on the face of the person holding them.

They quickly begin to recognise their main carer by the sound of his or her voice and through their own sense of smell.

They communicate by crying, but they soon cry in different ways for different reasons, e.g. hunger, boredom, tiredness.

At first, they have no voluntary control over their body. They cannot move from back to front. When lying on their backs, their head is usually on one side and, when on their stomachs, they usually lie with their knees tucked up, bottoms in the air and head to one side. Their hands are usually tightly closed.

Newborn babies do have a number of movements called reflexes. These are involuntary movements (ones that they cannot control) that are inborn and made automatically, and are important in helping the baby to survive. Most of these reflexes disappear by about three months.

The swallowing and sucking reflex

If a finger is placed in a baby's mouth, they will automatically suck and swallow – this helps them feed. Sometimes babies are born with sore fingers because they have sucked them in the womb.

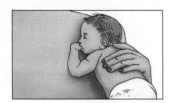

The rooting reflex

If a finger is gently stroked across the baby's cheek, they will automatically turn their heads towards it, as they search for a nipple or teat.

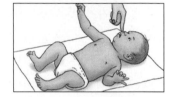

The grasping reflex

If an object or finger is placed in the palm of their hand, babies will automatically grasp it tightly.

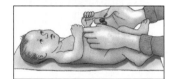

The walking reflex

If babies are held in a standing position, with the soles of their feet touching the floor, they will make stepping movements as if trying to walk.

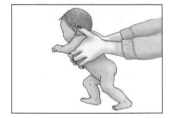

The startle reflex

If startled by a sudden bright light or a noise, babies will close their hand into a fist, bend their elbows and bring their arms towards their shoulders. They may also cry.

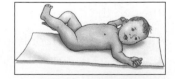

The falling reflex (Moro reflex)

Any sudden movement affecting the neck makes babies think they may be dropped. This makes them throw their arms back, and then bring them together as though they were trying to catch a ball.

Even in the first few weeks, newborn babies are beginning to learn about and understand their world. They do this through their senses – by looking, listening, touching, tasting and smelling. They soon begin to make noises other than crying and will soon enjoy kicking their legs and waving their hands, as well as communicating with people.

Physical development

Gross motor skills

- When held standing, will make walking or stepping movements.
- When lying on back (supine), head is turned to one side.
- When lying on tummy, the knees are tucked up, bottom is in the air and head is to one side.
- Limbs are curled up to body.
- Head is floppy.
- If held in a sitting position, head will 'lag' behind body.
- When held in a sitting position, back is rounded.

Fine motor skills

- If a finger or object is placed in their hand, they will grasp it tightly.
- Hands are usually closed.
- Thumb is often tucked under fingers.

Sensory skills

- Startled by sudden noises and bright lights.
- Turns towards sound.
- Begins to recognise main carer's voice.
- Cannot focus on objects more than 25 cm from eyes.
- Blinks at sudden bright lights.

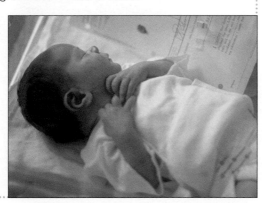

Intellectual – concepts

- Soon begins to recognise primary carer.
- On seeing primary carer will make excited movements with arms and legs, coo and smile.
- Will react to tone of voice of carer.

Intellectual – language

- Begins to cry in different ways depending on need, e.g. if hungry, tired, lonely.
- Begins to make different vocal noises, e.g. coos, gurgles, grunts.
- Begins to listen and tries to imitate sounds.
- Will watch lip movement if held face to face.
- Will start to respond with noises when spoken to.

Emotional and social development

- Begins to smile at carers.
- Will maintain eye contact when feeding.
- Turns towards carer's voice.

Three months

Babies are still completely dependent on other people. They are beginning to show more interest in their surroundings. Reflex actions are disappearing, and fine and gross motor skills are beginning to develop. They may begin to play with simple toys, such as a rattle, and communicate with smiles and gurgles.

Physical development

Gross motor skills
- When lying on front, can lift head and turn from side to side.
- When lying on front, can push up on arms and raise shoulders.
- Can kick legs strongly.
- If held in a sitting position, head will lag a little.
- When held, can sit with a straight back.

Fine motor skills
- Can hold a small toy for a short time before dropping.
- Looks at their hands and plays with hands and fingers.
- Grasp reflex may have disappeared.

Sensory skills
- Finds hands and brings them to mouth.
- Begins to move head to look at things when hearing a voice.
- Will turn towards a sound.
- Fascinated by faces.

Emotional development
- Becomes very attached to mother or main carer.
- Shows feelings and emotions.
- Shows pleasure when held.

Intellectual – concepts
- Becoming more aware of surroundings.
- Begins to use mouth to explore objects.
- May smile when spoken to by carer.
- Looks intently at things that move.

Intellectual – language
- Coos and gurgles to show contentment.
- May smile when spoken to by carer.
- May begin to babble.
- Beginning to control muscles of lips, tongue, voice box.

Social development
- Smiles both at family and strangers.
- Enjoys time with carers, e.g. bathtime and feeding.

Six months

By six months, babies can usually sit on their own for some time without support. They are becoming more interested and curious, and will explore everything they pick up by 'mouthing'. They enjoy being with people and being played with but are becoming unsure of strangers.

Physical development

Gross motor skills
- Can lift head and chest clear of floor using arms for support.
- Can sit for long periods if supported by cushions.
- Can sit for short periods without support but will 'topple' over.
- May try to roll over from back to front.
- May try to crawl.
- When lying on back, grasps legs and feet and puts feet into the mouth.
- Kicks strongly when lying on back.
- May hold out hands to be picked up.

Fine motor skills
- Puts all objects to mouth (mouthing).
- Grabs toys using whole hand (palmar grasp).
- Begins to reach out for small toys.
- Can pass toys from one hand to the other.
- Has learnt to drop things.

Sensory skills
- Still 'mouths' toys and objects.
- Looks around curiously.
- If a toy falls out of sight, will not look for it.
- Watches what people are doing.

Intellectual – language
- Cooing may cease.
- Babbling is more repetitive (e.g. 'da da da') and more tuneful (echolalia).
- Laughs, chuckles and squeals.
- Screams with annoyance.
- May understand simple words, e.g. 'bye-bye', 'mama'.
- Begins to imitate/repeat sounds.

Social development
- Enjoys being played with.
- May display separation anxiety.
- May be afraid of strangers.
- May feed using fingers.
- May begin to play with family members in a simple way, e.g. stroking face.
- May play alone (solitary play) with a simple toy, e.g. rattle.

Intellectual – concepts
- Knows to hold out arms to be picked up.
- Can recognise mother's or main carer's voice and will turn towards them.
- Spatial awareness is improving so may notice toys that are half hidden.

Emotional development
- Will enjoy being played with.
- Laughs with pleasure.
- May 'cling' to mother or main carer for security.

Nine months

Baby is now becoming more mobile and will be beginning to crawl or 'cruise'. Baby can now sit for long periods of time and reach for things without toppling over. Language skills are beginning to develop. Baby is usually shy with strangers.

Physical development

Gross motor skills

- Tries to crawl by rocking backwards and forwards.
- Can pull into a standing position by going onto knees first.
- May begin to sidestep (cruise) around furniture.
- Can stand when holding on to furniture.
- May begin to crawl upstairs.
- Can sit unsupported for longer periods of time.
- When sitting, can turn to look sideways and stretch to reach toys.
- May take some steps if held.

Fine motor skills

- Uses primitive pincer grasp (thumb and first finger) to pick up small objects.
- Can release a toy by dropping it but cannot put it down voluntarily.
- Will begin to look for dropped or fallen objects that are out of sight.
- Uses index finger to point.
- Pokes objects with index finger.

Sensory skills

- Looks in correct place for fallen or falling toys.
- Begins to recognise familiar pictures.
- Enjoys joining in games such as 'peek-a-boo'.

Intellectual – concepts

- Can tell the difference between family and strangers.
- Recognises familiar games and rhymes.
- Recognises own name and will turn head when spoken to.
- Has no concept of danger.
- May look for a toy they see being hidden (object permanence).

Intellectual – language

- Repeats syllables, e.g. 'dad dad', 'mum mum', 'ba ba'.
- Uses sound deliberately to express emotions.
- Imitates sounds, e.g. blows raspberries, smacks lips.
- May understand simple words, e.g. 'no', 'bye-bye'.

Social development

- May drink from a cup without help.
- Will still need to be close to a familiar adult.
- Will be happy to play alone.
- May hold out hands to be washed.

Emotional development

- May need a comfort object or toy to take to bed, e.g. teddy.
- May still show fear of strangers.

Twelve months

By twelve months, the world is becoming a bigger and more interesting place because children are now becoming more mobile as they learn to crawl and walk. Also at around this age, language development starts to 'take off'. Socially and emotionally, children will still be shy with others and need to be close to parents/carers.

Physical development

Gross motor skills
- Becoming very mobile – either by crawling, shuffling, 'bear walking' or bottom shuffling.
- Can cruise along furniture.
- Can walk a few steps if held.
- May start to walk but will tend to fall or sit suddenly.
- Can sit unsupported for long periods of time.
- Tries to crawl upstairs forwards and downstairs backwards.
- Can stand alone.

Fine motor skills
- Uses a neat pincer grasp (thumb and first finger) to pick up small objects.
- Points at objects of interest with index finger.
- Uses both hands, but may begin to show preference for one.
- Puts small objects into a container, e.g. bricks into a beaker.
- Drops and throws toys deliberately.
- Uses tripod grasp to hold bricks and bang them together.
- May hold a crayon in a palmar grasp.
- May try to turn pages in a book but usually several at once.

Sensory skills
- Watches people, animals and moving objects for long periods.
- Drops and throws toys deliberately, and watches them fall.
- Looks for lost or hidden toys.
- Recognises familiar people and sounds.
- Turns to sound.

Intellectual – concepts
- Is learning through trial and error.
- Will pick up toys and hand them to others, when asked.
- Can understand and act on simple instructions, e.g. 'wave bye-bye'.

Intellectual – language
- Imitates simple words.
- Recognises simple words and points, showing understanding.
- Babbling becomes more tuneful and similar to speech.
- Learns first words (active vocabulary).
- Understands more words than they can vocalise (passive vocabulary).
- Talks incessantly in their own language (jargon).

Social development
- Will still want to be close to familiar people.
- Enjoys others' company, especially at mealtimes.
- Uses fingers to feed themselves.
- May drink from a feeding cup by themselves.
- May help dressing by holding out leg/arm.

Emotional development
- Shows affection for parents and family.
- Needs to hold hands to feel secure.

Fifteen months

By fifteen months, children are much more mobile and can walk along unaided, although they may bump into furniture. Fine motor skills are developing well and they may enjoy simple drawing activities. They are still very egocentric, and learn through trial and error.

Physical development

Gross motor skills
- Walks independently, using arms to balance.
- Can crawl upstairs safely and downstairs feet first.
- Throws a large ball but may fall over.
- Can kneel without support.
- Can get up to a standing position without the help of people or furniture.

Fine motor skills
- Claps hands together.
- May build a tower of two blocks if shown how.
- Can pick up and drink from a cup using two hands to hold it.
- Can make a mark with a crayon using a palmar grasp.
- Turns pages in a book but will turn several at once.
- Tries to eat with a spoon but will turn it upside down.

Sensory skills
- Looks with interest at pictures in a book and pats them.
- Stands at a window and watches what is happening for long periods of time.

Intellectual – concepts
- Understands object permanence – that things exist even if they cannot be seen.
- Still very egocentric.
- More adventurous and wants to explore.
- Grasps crayon halfway up using palmar grasp with either hand.
- Scribbles to and fro.

Intellectual – language
- Uses several words that parents can understand.
- Points and uses single words to indicate an item.
- Beginning to use words to communicate.

Social development
- Becoming more helpful – will try to dress themselves but will need help.
- Can hold a cup and drink from it without help.
- May begin to understand when they want to go to the toilet but cannot control muscles.
- Still shy with strangers.

Emotional development
- Shows love and affection to family members.

Eighteen months

By this age, most children can walk well, are becoming more adventurous and want to explore, but have little understanding of danger. Fine motor skills are much improved and language skills are beginning to develop fast. They are becoming more sociable.

Physical development

Gross motor skills
- Can walk confidently and steadily without using arms to balance.
- Can pick up toys by bending from waist.
- Can 'squat' to look for things without losing balance.
- May be able to walk upstairs and downstairs without adult help.
- Runs, but sometimes bumps into obstacles.
- Can push and pull toys when walking.
- Can crawl backwards downstairs.

Fine motor skills
- Can turn knobs and handles on doors.
- Can build a tower of three bricks.
- Can string together large beads.
- Uses mature pincer grasp to pick up objects.
- Beginning to use the tripod grasp when using pencils and crayons.
- Can pull off shoes.
- Fascinated by buttons, zips and other fastenings.

Sensory skills
- Hand–eye coordination is good.
- Can pick up small objects, such as beads, on sight with delicate pincer grasp.
- Enjoys simple picture books.
- Recognises and points to brightly coloured items on a page.
- Recognises familiar people at a distance.

Social development
- Becoming more sociable.
- May refuse to obey instructions.
- Still egocentric and shy of strangers, needing a familiar adult close to them.
- Plays happily alone (solitary play).
- May enjoy playing alongside others (parallel play).
- Can use a cup and spoon well.
- Can take off clothing quite easily and help to dress themselves.
- Can give warning that they need the toilet by words and actions.

Intellectual – concepts
- Can recognise and point to pictures in a book if asked.
- Memory is developing.
- When drawing, uses scribbles and dots.
- Tries to imitate adult actions.
- Starts to match shapes to holes in a shape sorter.
- Knows and can point to parts of the body.
- Recognises objects from books and pictures.
- May start to do simple jigsaws.

Intellectual – language
- Active vocabulary increases.
- Words are used to mean more than one thing, e.g. 'cup' may mean 'Where is my cup?', 'I want my cup', 'I've dropped my cup'.
- Echoes and repeats words (echolalia).
- Enjoys trying to copy rhymes and simple songs.
- Words are symbolic, e.g. 'dog' is used for any four-legged animal (holophrases).

Emotional development
- Will show different and strong emotions, e.g. fear, anger, happiness.
- May change from negative to positive emotions quickly.
- Becoming more independent.

AQA HOME ECONOMICS FOR GCSE: CHILD DEVELOPMENT – CONTROLLED ASSESSMENT GUIDE

Two years

At this age, children can run, walk and talk and are becoming more independent. They are curious and want to explore but still have only limited understanding of danger. When frustrated or stopped from doing something, they throw temper tantrums. Pretend play is important at this stage.

Physical development

Gross motor skills

- Can walk upstairs and downstairs confidently, two feet to a step.
- Enjoys climbing on furniture.
- Can kick a large ball that is not moving.
- Enjoys toys that are put together and pulled apart.
- Walks and runs more safely and steadily.
- Pushes and pulls large-wheeled toys.
- Can sit on a tricycle and use feet to move it.

Fine motor skills

- Can turn pages of a book one by one.
- Has good hand–eye coordination.
- Can build a tower of five or six bricks.
- Uses mature pincer grasp to pick up and position small objects.
- Holds a pencil firmly and can form circles, lines and dots.
- Can zip and unzip large zippers.
- Uses preferred hand.

Sensory skills

- Enjoys looking at picture books.
- Recognises fine detail in favourite pictures.
- Recognises familiar adults in photographs.

Intellectual – concepts

- May make a letter V when drawing.
- Vertical lines and circular scribble forming.
- May begin to sort and match.
- Uses symbolic play, e.g. a twig from a tree will become a sword.
- Still very egocentric.
- Enjoys books.
- Learns by copying and imitating adults.

Emotional development

- Will act out feelings and ideas through pretend play.
- Will have tantrums and show strong emotions when frustrated.
- Becoming more independent but will still often cling to an adult.
- May still display separation anxiety.

Intellectual – language

- Is learning new words quickly.
- Has a larger vocabulary.
- May use telegraphic sentences, e.g. 'Me want ball'.
- Beginning to use pronouns, e.g. 'me', 'I', 'you'.
- Beginning to ask questions.
- Talks non-stop.
- Begins to use negatives, e.g. 'no teddy'.

Social development

- Will play near other children (parallel play).
- Still finds it hard to share.
- Can feed without too much mess and uses a spoon well.
- Can lift a cup and put it down without spilling.
- By two and a half, may be able to pour a drink for themselves.
- Can put on some clothing themselves.
- By two and a half, can unfasten buttons, zips and buckles.
- Can say when they need the toilet.
- By two and a half, should be dry during the day; may be dry at night.

Three years

By this age, children are much more independent and confident. They become less frustrated when trying to do things because they are becoming more skilful, so temper tantrums are less frequent. They are trusting and more sociable, so will play with others and enjoy creative and pretend play.

Physical development

Gross motor skills
- Can walk and run forwards with precision.
- Can walk on tiptoe.
- Can kick a ball forwards.
- Can throw overhand.
- Can catch a large ball with extended arms.
- Can pedal and steer a tricycle.
- Can walk upstairs with one foot on each step.
- Can hop on one foot.
- Can manoeuvre around objects, showing spatial awareness.

Fine motor skills
- Holds a crayon with more control and can draw a face.
- Can eat with a spoon or fork without spilling food.
- Can colour in more neatly and within the lines.
- Can put on and take off coat.
- Can build a tower of nine or ten bricks.
- Cuts with toy scissors.
- Uses improved tripod grasp.

Sensory skills
- Knows name of some colours.
- Can match two or three main colours, usually red and yellow.
- Listens eagerly to favourite stories and wants to hear them over and over again.
- Can thread large beads.

Intellectual – concepts
- Beginning to understand concept of time – especially past and future.
- Beginning to understand number concept of 1 and lots.
- Beginning to use language to describe thoughts and ideas.
- Can count up to ten by rote.
- Enjoys music, both making it and listening to it.
- Concentrates for longer periods of time.
- Understands concepts of cause and effect.
- Enjoys pretend play.
- Can copy a circle but does not always join it up.
- May write letters V, H and T.
- Draws a head with one or two features.

Intellectual – language
- Vocabulary is large.
- Sentences are longer and close to adult speech.
- Often holds long, imaginary conversations when playing.
- Incessantly asks questions: why, when, where, what?
- May use incorrect word endings, e.g. 'drawed', 'sheeps'.

Emotional development
- Shows feelings and concern for others.
- Sometimes develops fears, e.g. of the dark.
- Temper tantrums are not as frequent.
- May have outgrown separation anxiety.

Social development

- Can use a fork and spoon to eat.
- Will go to the toilet on their own during day.
- Should be dry at night.
- Can wash their hands but not dry them properly.
- Becoming independent – wanting to dress themselves.
- Will begin to show interest in other children and to play with them (joining-in play).
- More trusting.

Four years

By this age, gross and fine motor skills are quite well developed. Children are creative and imaginative, and enjoy making things. Language skills are good – they enjoy playing with other children, can usually take turns and may begin to understand rules. They are curious and love to explore and investigate.

Physical development

Gross motor skills
- Can walk or run alone, and walk upstairs and downstairs, in adult fashion.
- Can walk along a straight line showing good balance.
- Can climb ladders and trees.
- Pedals and controls a tricycle confidently.
- Is becoming more skilled at ball games – can throw, catch, bounce and kick a ball, and use a bat.

Fine motor skills
- Can build a tower of ten or more blocks.
- Can build three steps with six bricks, if shown how.
- Uses a mature pincer grasp.
- Can fasten and unfasten buttons.
- Can put together large-piece jigsaws.
- Can colour in pictures, but not always within the lines.

Sensory skills
- Can match and name four main colours.
- Follows story books with eyes and identifies words and pictures.

Intellectual – language
- May use about 1,500 words.
- Talks about past and future.
- Sentences are more grammatically correct but may still get endings wrong.
- Uses a variety of questions.
- Uses positional words, e.g. in, over, under.
- May mispronounce words.
- May mix up sounds like 'th' and 'f'.

Social development
- Will begin to play with others (cooperative play).
- Will play alone for long periods without adult attention.
- Will share and take turns.
- Can feed themselves skilfully.
- Can dress and undress.
- Can wash and dry hands and face, and clean teeth.

Intellectual – concepts
- Can count up to ten by rote.
- Beginning to understand number concept 1–3.
- Understands concept of past and future.
- Still muddles fact with fiction.
- Enjoys jokes.
- Can repeat songs and rhymes without mistakes.
- May know letters of the alphabet.
- Beginning to understand concept of right and wrong.
- Can concentrate for longer periods.
- May be able to copy letters V, H, T and O.
- Begins to trace shapes, letters and numbers formed by dots.
- Draws a 'potato person' with head, legs and trunk.
- Figures drawn may not have fingers or toes on arms or legs.

Emotional development
- Will be very affectionate towards family friends and people they see often.
- More trusting.
- Will tell their thoughts and feelings to people.
- Shows love for younger brothers or sisters.

Five years

By this age, most children's physical skills are well developed and they are becoming more agile and skilful. Language and communication skills are also well developed. They enjoy imaginary games and team games, understanding the need for rules, and can cooperate with others.

Physical development

Gross motor skills
- Can skip with a rope.
- Very skilful at climbing, sliding, swinging, jumping, etc.
- Can use a wide variety of large equipment confidently.
- Can throw a ball to a partner, and catch and hit a ball with a bat with some accuracy.
- Can balance on one foot for several seconds.
- Can hop on each foot.
- Can dance rhythmically to music.

Fine motor skills
- Dresses and undresses with little help.
- Can complete more complex jigsaws with interlocking pieces.
- Can cut out shapes using scissors more accurately.
- Can use a knife and fork when eating.
- Has good pencil control.
- Can colour in pictures neatly, staying within outlines.
- Can construct complex models using kits.
- Can copy several letters, e.g. V, T, H, O, X, L, A, C, O and Y.

Sensory skills
- Matches 10–12 colours.
- Vision and hearing developing to adult level.

Intellectual – concepts
- Can distinguish between fact and fiction.
- Begins to understand the concept of measurement.
- Can count up to 20 by rote.
- Uses reasoning based on experience.
- Can understand right and wrong.
- Can understand simple rules and the need for them.
- Talks about past, present and future.
- May begin to read.
- Recognises name when written and tries to write it.
- Can copy squares, triangles and letters V, T, H, O, X, G, A, U and Y.
- May write own name and simple words.
- Can draw a house with windows, door, chimney and roof.
- Pictures now have a background, e.g. sky.
- Draws a person and head with one or two features.
- Can copy a circle but might not join it up.

Social development
- May start to play more with own sex.
- Beginning to choose own friends.
- Will play happily with other children.
- Can pick up and replace very small objects.

Emotional development
- Helps and comforts other children who are unhappy or hurt.
- Will respond to reasoning.
- Can still be selfish.

Intellectual – language
- Speech is grammatically correct and more fluent.
- Enjoys jokes and riddles.

Suitable toys and play for different ages

Children play in a variety of ways and with different toys. All types of play will help their development in some way.

Age	Toys and play
Birth to three months	**Toys:** Mobiles above or attached to cot. Soft toys and balls. Rattles, teething rings and other hand-held toys that are safe to put into mouth. Young babies should be held close, talked or sung to often. **Play:** At this age, babies enjoy social play, such as 'peek-a-boo', as they learn to bond with carers. Towards three months, they will enjoy sensory play and finger play, which helps develop fine motor skills.
Six months	**Toys:** As for three months, plus activity centres, non-breakable mirrors, activity mats with textures and hidden noises, bath toys, cardboard boxes to put toys in, simple picture books, things to bang, playing 'peek-a-boo' and 'this little piggy'. **Play:** Are often happy to play with simple toys alone – solitary play.
Nine months	**Toys:** As for six months, plus rattles and toys that will stick to surfaces, balls of different sizes and textures, stacking toys, fabric, card or plastic books, large soft bricks, feely bags or boxes. Will enjoy songs and rhymes with actions, e.g. 'pat-a-cake'. **Play:** Although still mainly enjoy solitary play, they may be happy watching others. Play is mainly physical as their gross and fine motor skills develop.
Twelve months	**Toys:** As for nine months, plus musical toys and boxes, simple jigsaws, bricks and containers, push and pull toys, picture books with simple rhymes, 'hide-and-seek' games. Will also enjoy sand and water play, play dough and copying adults, e.g. dusting. **Play:** Is still mainly looking-on play but they are becoming more aware of other people and will 'play with them', e.g. pass things backwards and forwards.
Fifteen months	**Toys:** As for twelve months, plus soft balls to throw, building bricks, cause and effect toys, e.g. jack-in-the-box, drawing and simple gluing activities, listening to nursery rhymes and stories, dancing to music. **Play:** Enjoy a lot of physical play as their fine and gross motor skills improve.
Eighteen months	**Toys:** As for fifteen months, plus shape sorters, hammering toys, toy telephones, play dough, musical toys, books with joining-in activities, simple story books. Will enjoy simple sticking and gluing, modelling and finger painting, circle games, e.g. 'ring-a-ring-a-roses' and songs and rhymes with actions. **Play:** Most play is still looking-on play but may start to enjoy parallel play. Will often try to copy others.

Age	Toys and play
Two years	**Toys:** As for eighteen months, plus dressing-up clothes, construction toys, dolls and teddies for pretend play, musical toys, e.g. xylophone. Outdoor toys could include simple climbing frames, small slides and swings, sit and ride toys, paddling pools. May enjoy painting and colouring-in and simple printing. **Play:** Enjoy parallel play – playing alongside other children but not really with them. They often like having the same toy as other children but will not play or share with them. Beginning to enjoy pretend play.
Three years	**Toys:** As for two years, plus small world toys, pop-up books or books with lift-up flaps. Simple cooking, drawing and painting, building things. Will enjoy making 'dens', helping in the house, matching and sorting games, riding tricycle. **Play:** Begin to enjoy playing with other children, joining-in play, and are more independent. A lot of their play is imaginative/pretend play.
Four years	**Toys:** As for three years, plus counting and alphabet games, making collages, junk modelling, messy and creative play, simple board games, card games, e.g. snap, dressing-up and imaginative play. Outdoor toys could include skipping ropes, footballs, obstacle courses, toy gardening tools. **Play:** Enjoy all types of play, such as outdoor physical play, pretend, discovery and creative play. May start to enjoy cooperative play and to share and take turns.
Five years	**Toys:** As for four years, plus more complex painting and drawing activities and jigsaws. Games with rules, books with more characters and detailed stories and pictures. Outdoors, will enjoy team games, large climbing frames, mini-trampolines, hopscotch, catch and chase. **Play:** Enjoy playing with others (cooperative play) and understand about taking turns and simple rules. They love to explore and investigate and also sometimes still like playing alone.

Appendix

Unit 2: the research task (20 per cent)

Name _____ Start date _____ Completion date _____

Chosen task _____

Steps	Evidence		Tick
Step 1 Analyse the chosen task	Write down what the task is asking you to do		
	State the information you need to find		
Step 2 Planning the research	State what you hope to find out		
	Primary research		
	Secondary research		
	Presentation of information		
Step 3 Carrying out the research	Action plan		
	Carry out research		
	Primary research, e.g. questionnaire, survey, etc.	Secondary research, e.g. books, internet, etc.	
Step 4 Analysing and evaluating	Primary research analysed		
	Secondary research analysed		
	Evaluation of research		
Step 5 Planning the outcome	Type of outcome, e.g. leaflet		
	Purpose/focus of leaflet		
	Target group		
	Analysis of existing leaflet		
	Plan of leaflet/sketch		
	Presentation ideas		
Step 6 Making outcome	Produce actual outcome, e.g. leaflet, booklet		
Step 7 Final analysis and evaluation	Success of outcome		
	Outcome tested on target group		
	Improvements		
	Bibliography		

Unit 2: the child study (40 per cent)

Name _____ Start date _____ Completion date _____

Chosen research task _____

Choosing the child	Child must be under the age of five at the **end** of the study		
Steps	**Evidence**		**Tick**
Step 1 Introductory visit	Age of child: _____ years _____ months		
	Physical description	Physical development	
	Family background	Intellectual	
	Home/local area	Emotional	
	Personality	Social	
	Play	Conclusion	
Step 2 Choosing an AQA task	Write out chosen task		
Step 3 Planning and doing the research	Planning the task		
	Carry out research		
	Primary research, e.g. questionnaire, survey, etc.	Secondary research, e.g. books, internet, etc.	
Step 4 Evaluating the research	Analysis of importance of primary research		
	Analysis of importance of secondary research		
	Overall evaluation of research		
	How research will be used to plan visits		
Step 5 Planning **four** visits	Dates of visits		
	Activities listed		
	Two visits linked to research		
Step 6 Carry out **four** visits	Visit 1	Date:	
	Visit 2	Date:	
	Visit 3	Date:	
	Visit 4	Date:	
Step 7 Final evaluation	Final evaluation of:		
	Physical		
	Intellectual		
	Emotional		
	Social		
	Evaluation of research and activities		
	Bibliography		
	Appendix		

Possible layout for writing up visits

Date of visit:

Age of child: (Give the same information for each visit, e.g. years and months)

Place:

Length of visit:

Aims and planning:

Expectations/predictions:

Observation:

Evaluation:

Ideas for activities

Imaginative play	Social play	Creative play
• Dressing up • Small world • Making dens • Cooking • Puppet shows	• Tea party with other children • Board games that involve taking turns • Dressing up games • Any game that requires cooperation and sharing • Visiting a soft play area	• Making a collage • Painting • Drawing • Modelling with salt dough/play dough • Making a card
Junk modelling	**Cutting and sticking**	**Painting, drawing and printing**
• Animals from a cereal box • Doll's house from a shoe box • Car from a large cardboard box	• Making a card for a special occasion • Making a mask • Mosaics from old, coloured magazines	• Finger painting • Block painting • Printing with hands and feet or fruit and vegetables • Dot-to-dot drawings
Construction toys	**Small world play**	**Food and cooking**
Observing the child: • playing with Duplo®, Lego® or Sticklebricks® • creating their own models from junk	• Trains • Playmobil® • Doll's house • Zoo/farm animals	• Making a book about healthy food • Shopping trip to the supermarket to buy healthy food • Eating plate • Making and baking food • Preparing healthy snacks and drinks • Having picnics • Visiting a café
Colour	**Shape**	**Number**
• Painting and mixing colours • Painting by numbers • Reading a book about colours	• Playing with shapes sorters with very young children • Using play/salt dough to roll and cut out shapes • Making and copying 3D shapes • Reading a book together about shapes • Looking at the shapes of everyday objects	• Songs and rhymes, e.g. 'ten green bottles', 'round and round the garden' • Playing board games using dice • Playing dominoes • Shopping games • Designing an activity book, e.g. dot-to-dot

Books	Pretend play	Music and dancing
• Interactive • Talking • Flapbooks • Making books • Reading • Going to a library	• Small world play, e.g. hospital, school, farm • Making a car from a cardboard box and using it to visit the beach • Making a play or story using puppets and performing to friends or family • Playing cafés, waiting to be served, or serving	• Action songs on TV or DVD • Dancing to music • Exercising to music • Making and using musical instruments from household products • Performing a song to a parent/sibling • Playing with a toy karaoke • Dressing up and having a disco party

Words that connect or start sentences

In writing up your coursework, the following words might be useful. They either **connect** or **start** sentences.

First(ly)…	Also…	In particular…
Second(ly)…	Moreover…	Above all…
Then…	As a result…	Notably…
…and then…	Equally…	Specifically…
…after(wards)…	Similarly…	…especially…
Meanwhile…	Likewise…	
During…	In the same way…	For example…
Whenever…	As with…	…such as…
Eventually…	As a result…	
Finally…		Clearly…
	However…	…of course…
In addition…	…but…	…the following…
Furthermore…	Nevertheless…	
Therefore…	Alternatively…	In brief…
Consequently…	Despite this…	On the whole…
…because/as…	…instead…	To sum up…
accordingly…	Whereas…	In conclusion…
…as long as…	Although…	

Some useful words and phrases

Physical		Intellectual	Emotional	Social
Gross motor	**Fine motor**			
balancing	ambidextrous	acquire	anxiety	aggressive
bear-walking	building	babbling	attention	attachment
bending	clutching	communicating	bonding	attention
bouncing	cutting out	concentrating	boredom	seeking
catching	dressing	concepts	comforter	attitudes
clapping	fastening	copying	confidence	behaviour
climbing	zipper/button	creative	control	bladder control
coordination	fine muscular	curious	defiant	caring
crawling	control	echolalia	dummy	cleaning teeth
cruising	grasping	egocentric	excitable	considerate
dancing	hand–eye	encourage	excitement	cooperative play
hopping	coordination	experience	fear	cultural
jumping	inferior pincer	exploring	feelings	curious
kicking	grasp	genes	frustration	friendly
lifting	interlocking	imagining	happiness	independence
muscular	joining	imitating	jealous	joining in
pedalling	left-handed	independent	love	manners
running	making	investigating	moody	parallel (play)
shuffling	mature pincer	jargon	nail biting	please
sitting	grasp	knowledge	negative	polite
skipping	modelling	language	emotion	regression
sliding	palmar grasp	learning	nightmare	separation
squatting	passing	listening	positive emotion	anxiety
standing	picking up	looking	praise	share
stirring	pincer grasp	nature and	sadness	shy
swimming	placing	nurture	scared	social skill
swinging	pointing	object	scream	solitary (play)
throwing	posting	permanence	self-confidence	stranger
twisting	primitive tripod	perception	self-image	take turns
walking	grasp	questions	self-esteem	thank you
	reflex	remember	separation	toilet training
	right-handed	stimulate	anxiety	washing hands
	sticking	talking	shriek	
	stringing	telegraphic	stress	
	threading	sentences	temper	
	tripod grasp	understand	tantrums	
	turning (pages)		temperament	
			thumb sucking	
			worry	

Ideas for outcomes

AQA HOME ECONOMICS FOR GCSE: CHILD DEVELOPMENT – CONTROLLED ASSESSMENT GUIDE

Index